MINDLESS BEHAVIORS

Breaking through Unseen Barriers

BEATRICE ADENODI

Minneapolis

ISBN 13: 978-1-63489-376-3

Library of Congress Catalog Number: 2020915062
Printed in the United States of America
First Printing: 2021

23 22 21 20 21   5 4 3 2 1

Book design by Patrick Maloney

Wise Ink Creative Publishing
807 Broadway St NE
Suite 46
Minneapolis, MN, 55413

CONTENTS

INTRODUCTION

I remember sitting in history classes as a child and studying different wars. Each year, I learned about conflicts that repeated themselves in different times and places, divisions that needlessly isolated groups from each other. I learned about racism, struggle, heartbreak, violence, deception, manipulation, dependency, segregation, disconnection, unfairness, and judgment, all before the age of eighteen. The message I took away was that humans are steeped in biases from such a young age that we replicate what we see throughout our lives. Lessons about how we might overcome these biases and mend our divisions were few and far between.

Most humans live their lives on the shoreline, boxing themselves in with self-limiting beliefs. All this does is keep us wrapped in a beach towel of placid contentment with an inability to swim out to the deep waters, to explore our ultimate potential and learn what's keeping us stuck. We play, build, and expand on the shores, advancing this complacent mindset through successive generations. Over time, people cling ever more tightly to traditions, systems, institutions, social norms, and inherited beliefs that, while "safe," no longer serve them. All these systems and beliefs in turn create communication barriers, making it difficult for people to understand others' perceptions and viewpoints.

It's challenging to communicate across cultures if you feel there are "right" or "wrong" ways to live. It's also hard to create an identity for yourself when you're handed one from your family, social group, religion, and so on. Think about it: Everything we learn in school is based on one account of how one person or group did something. Our family traditions are based on what worked for the generations before us. Our social norms are based on what the masses think is acceptable. In every aspect of our lives we're part of the same systems, trying to find answers through the same processes that created our questions.

This book explores different issues that manifest when questions around our identities and beliefs are left unanswered. It also illustrates how unconscious our behaviors become when we're disconnected from the core of who we are. Subconsciously, mindless behaviors make us forget our shared humanity, make us mistreat each other, and blind us to our true potential.

Our environments affect the way we operate, and unconscious behaviors are an immediate reaction to the situations we're exposed to. Most of our lives these days are spent in environments where we're simply surviving from moment to moment, reacting instead of reflecting. As a result, our world is conditional—personal and professional bonds can be formed and dissolved at will.

My Journey to Awakening the God Within

In 2013, I decided to take a permanent role at a software company. It wasn't exactly the role I was looking for, but after tirelessly looking for a stable job, I thought it would be best to put my big girl pants on and conform to the rest of the world. I wanted more; I just didn't know how to articulate what "more" looked like in my personal and professional life.

After many signs that I was sliding down a rabbit hole of disinterest, one day a question hit me: "How did I get here?" At the time, I pondered this question, but I didn't fully address it. And the more I worked and ignored the gnawing anxiety in my gut, the more lost I became as time progressed.

One day, I was training several employees at one of our client companies on how to use a product I represented. When I looked around the room, I noticed nearly everyone was either texting on their phones, looking around aimlessly, or chatting—in other words, doing everything but listening to me, even though they were the ones who asked me to come to their offices.

At the time, I was debating whether to keep my job or let it go, and generally trying to figure out what I wanted to do with my life. So when I looked around that room, I said to myself, "Why am I here?" And then, "I don't want to do this anymore."

The employees couldn't have known what I was going through, but they were victims of my pain, which was spilling over them unconsciously. I was lost and bleeding from every part of my life, to the point I'd become a stranger to myself. In addition to working ninety-hour weeks, I was constantly aiding my friends, who always seemed to need help; trying to mend a relationship with an ex; and supporting my aging parents. As a result, I didn't have time to process what I was experiencing or even take care of my mental health.

What I realized was that most of life is spent simply surviving with a mindset of scarcity. It's urgent to have an in-depth conversation about situations that keep us stuck. In my case, I had to stop taking on other people's problems and focus on fixing my own.

Back then, I clung to everything but my own beliefs. I unconsciously gave my power away through the way I reacted to situations, what I did for people, and the way I enabled bad behaviors in those close to me. In time, my actions took a toll, reaching a breaking point one night when I let my friends persuade me to go somewhere I didn't belong. They knew if I showed up, it would spark a bit of a negative reaction, and it did. It wasn't the first time this had happened, but it was more painful than all the other times because I realized they were unaware of the trauma they were inflicting on me. But in my toughest moment, I discovered the potential inside me. For the first time, the smoke and mirrors started to clear. Another perspective started to seep into my consciousness, changing my life forever.

Dead-end jobs, toxic relationships, emotional barriers, blind faith, fear-based choices—I understand standing on the shorelines of life so well. Before I turned my life around, I went where I was tolerated and excelled at being less than my perfect—the ultimate soldier of a slave system that kept me bound to an invisible rat race. Comfort kept me wrapped in my beliefs. It felt safer not to venture into the ocean because I feared being judged. I also loved pleasing everyone around me; I loved helping people any way I could because deep down, it made me feel valuable.

I was living a life I didn't want, communicating in a way that didn't serve my truth, and struggling with a mindset that kept me stuck. I was a walking mindless behavior. (Although I realized some of my actions weren't entirely my fault; I inherited a lot of my behaviors from family, through education, and in the systems I grew up with.)

Over four years, I set out on a journey to better understand how I communicate with myself and the world around me. I discovered the God within me by acknowledging my shortcomings and building self-awareness. By relying on my innate wisdom, I learned that a limited mind only produces limited results.

What Are Mindless Behaviors?

The term "mindless behaviors" applies to two things. The first are deeply ingrained behavioral patterns that can be barriers to personal growth: enabling bad behavior, living with masks, and so on.

Mindless Behaviors (note the capitals) is also a social experiential platform that strives to build community awareness of these behaviors. Through our social experiences, we connect individuals with their inner voice to create a pathway to emotional intelligence and a stronger sense of identity. Our platform offers effective communication tools that enable people to increase self-awareness and implement problem-solving tactics in everyday life. We create thought-provoking conversations that open individuals' minds to new perspectives, guiding them from being reactive to being reflective.

Through exposure to hurtful, traumatic, and counter-productive life experiences (family systems, educational systems, through the media, and so on), we've learned to engage in a cycle: react, avoid, and suffer. We react to our environment with hostility instead of responding in proactive ways that align with who we are. We avoid understanding and addressing tough situations. Instead, we adopt facades such as "everything's fine" and "I don't need help"; blame ourselves ("It's my fault," "I deserved this"); or blame others ("I feel this way because of him/her/them"). As a result, we suffer in our relationships with others and with ourselves.

In this cycle of reacting, avoiding, and suffering, we forget the root causes of our pain over time. We stay stuck in this physical, mental, and emotional cycle because we haven't learned to understand our experiences, examine ourselves honestly, and practice problem-solving in our lives. We can start empowering ourselves and communicating more effectively with one another by being more intentional in our everyday actions, which is the aim of this book: to enhance your behavioral knowledge to help you get unstuck and become more deliberate in your actions.

Why I Wrote This Book

This book brings to life thought-provoking viewpoints that are different takes on our usual way of living and approaching problems. It will help you unblock areas of your life that feel cluttered and enhance your ability to awaken the God within you.

Through my personal, professional, and social experiences, I've learned that most of life's problems are really just different versions of the same handful of problems. Undeniably, there are patterns that regularly wreak havoc on our lives. This book sheds light on the negative cycles that impact the human condition and the importance of effective communication in breaking them.

Through seven different stories that examine life through the lens of Mindless Behaviors, you'll learn that if you change the way you perceive your circumstances and actions, you have the power to change your life forever. It's my hope that you'll read this book and gain a new perspective, acknowledge your shortcomings and unconscious biases, and shed light on activating your untapped potential.

Chapter One

THE MASKS WE WEAR

Tick-tock-tick-tock! Peter, his hands shaking on the armrests of his chair, watched the clock. At three, he would give the biggest speech of his life on national TV.

"What's wrong?" Tiara said as she slowly put on his makeup. "I've never seen you this nervous in all the years I've worked for you. You love going on stage!"

"I'm fine," Peter said. "I just have a lot going on. It's nothing." He forced a smile, hoping Tiara believed him.

She smiled gently. "Okay. Whatever you say, boss."

When Tiara was finished, Peter went to the green room to practice his speech. It was now 1:30 p.m., and the anxiety was creeping back in like a snake slithering into a garden on a sunny day. Every minute closer to three made Peter's heart throb.

Peter was pacing when his wife, Laura, walked in.

"Hi, honey! Ready for your speech?" she asked.

"Hey, what a surprise!" Peter said. "You never come to my speeches."

"Well, I just thought you needed some extra support today. You've seemed a bit off lately."

Peter smiled. "Thank you, love! You being here makes me feel a lot better."

"Are you going to tell me what's wrong?" Laura asked.

Peter's smile faded. "I'll tell you everything after the speech. I just need to get this off my plate. I'm addressing some issues that will affect the entire community."

"Okay, let's talk tonight. How about I make dinner?" Laura said.

"Sure!"

There was a quick knock on the door, and then the stage manager poked her head in. "Sorry to interrupt, but it's ten minutes to showtime. We need to mic you up."

"Okay," Peter said. There was no turning back now; it was time to face his fate. He turned and kissed Laura on the cheek. "We'll talk tonight. I promise," he whispered.

She nodded, her eyes wide with concern.

He followed the stage manager backstage. After a few quick adjustments, Peter was wired for sound. It was three minutes to showtime.

"Do you need anything?" the stage manager said.

"No, I'm fine," Peter said.

One minute till showtime. As Peter walked across the stage to the podium, it felt as if bricks were tied to his feet. His hands trembled and his heart throbbed. He glanced over to see Laura standing at the edge of the stage, smiling at him.

The camera lights clicked and flashed uncontrollably as a sea of reporters raised their mics. In his earbud, Peter heard the stage manager: "Five, four, three, two, one—Peter, you're on!"

"Good afternoon, ladies and gentlemen. I regret to inform you that I, Peter Sherman, will resign from my position as senator effective immediately. This decision was challenging to make, but I feel it's the right course of action for me and my family. I thank you all for supporting me and allowing me to be of service to you and your communities. As the saying goes, all good things must come to an end. It is with great joy and peace that I start this new chapter, taking everything I've learned over the years as well as many wonderful memories. I love all of you from the bottom of my heart. Thank you so much and have a great afternoon."

Silence came over the room for a split second—then the questions rolled in. Peter stepped away from the podium and began to walk off stage. As he did, Laura stood in shock. They both locked eyes—then Laura ran off.

Before he could follow her, Tiffany, Peter's publicist, stormed up to him. "What the hell's going on? This is a PR crisis. We need to huddle in the green room, now!"

"Okay, okay," Peter shouted above the noise.

Tiffany pulled Peter to the green room, a throng of reporters surrounding them the entire way. When they got there, a few of the bolder journalists tried to push their way in, but Tiffany quickly locked the door. She heaved a sigh of relief before wheeling on Peter. "So, you want to tell me what happened?"

"I quit," said Peter. "It's as simple as that. I don't want to be a senator anymore."

"You just can't quit being a senator!" Tiffany screamed. "This state depends on you! What about your image? Your reputation?"

"I don't care about that stuff anymore. I care about my health and family." Peter stood. "You know what? I've made my decision. End of story." Before she could answer, he'd stormed out of the room.

The reporters and camera people followed him out of the building all the way to his car. Before getting inside, Peter turned and said, "I've already told you everything you need to know. I have no further comments." Then he hopped in and left, driving as fast as he could out of the parking lot.

After a few minutes on the road hunched over the wheel, he felt his shoulders relax—he was finally free! The heavy feeling in his heart lifted. He drove around aimlessly for hours, dreading the consequences of his sudden decision. His phone was ringing off the hook. He picked it up and considered it, then shut it off. *I just need to breathe.*

He pulled up to a Hilton outside the city at eleven o'clock. After getting a room for the night, he threw himself onto the king-sized bed and gazed at the celling, wondering what his next steps should be. He pulled out a bottle of rum he'd picked up on the drive and began to drink.

Sitting in silence, Peter remembered how dreadful it had been to make that life-changing announcement. But it was nothing compared to the thought that he must now face Laura and the rest of his family. Thousands of thoughts swirled in his mind until he finally fell into a deep, dreamless sleep.

————

The bright sunlight pierced through the window the following morning. Peter woke up looking for the clock. It was 9:00 a.m.

"Shit!" he said. He immediately got dressed, checked out, and hopped into his car to head home. On the way, Peter felt the same anxiety he'd had during his speech. Heart throbbing, palms sweating, he drove anxiously to confront his loved ones.

When he pulled into the driveway, Laura came running out of the house. As he got out of the car, she folded him into a hug.

"Thank god you're okay!" she said. "I was worried sick."

"I'm sorry," said Peter. "I just needed some time to clear my head, so I checked into a hotel."

Laura shook her head as she pulled him into the house. "Peter, this is so unlike you, spending the night at some hotel and not telling me where you are. And that announcement—just when did you plan to tell me you were quitting the Senate?"

"I started to tell you a thousand times," he said. "I just couldn't find the courage to follow through."

"So you decided to do it in public?" she yelled. She began pacing around their living room. "I was so embarrassed! I came to support you only to find out I wasn't part of a life-changing decision for our family. I found out when the rest of the world did. How do you think that made me feel? I'm your wife, Peter! We're supposed to be a team and I don't even know you anymore!" Laura threw herself onto a couch and started sobbing. "How did we get here?"

Peter sat beside her. "I'm sorry, honey. I haven't been honest with you. The truth is, I've been unhappy with my job for a long time. The stress, the long days and sleepless nights, the constant worry I'm not making a real impact. I felt like I was suffocating, drowning in my own life."

"Why didn't you tell me all this before?" she asked, sitting up and wiping away tears. "We could've worked it out."

"I needed to figure things out on my own," Peter said. "I've been thinking a lot about what kind of work I might actually enjoy. One of the things I loved as a kid was sculpting. I could get lost for hours shaping and chiseling blocks of clay. It was my escape from all the pressure I felt growing up. You know my family: there's been a Sherman in Louisiana state government for generations. I thought I should follow in their footsteps and make everyone proud, so I gave up sculpting when I went to college. My parents didn't give me a hard time about it; they never thought I could make a living as an artist anyway, so they were thrilled when I quit."

Laura's face softened. "You never told me you were an artist. I had no idea." She sat back and gave him a quizzical look. "When I first met you, you were so into politics and organizing that it was practically your whole life. What happened?"

Peter sighed. "Growing up, I supported my family in every one of our campaigns because it was all I knew. Being an artist was miles away from what my parents thought was 'normal,' and heaven forbid I disobey them—they would've cut me out of the family in a heartbeat. Besides, when you're young, all you want to do is please people. But as time went on, I realized that making my parents happy wasn't the only way to live a fulfilling life. Also . . ."

Peter stared at the floor, avoiding Laura's eyes. "That accident nine months ago—it changed me."

"Accident?" Laura said. "You mean the night you almost skidded into that ditch? But that was nothing. You said it yourself, the road was slippery because of the rain."

He shook his head. "It was pretty treacherous out, yes, but I didn't tell you the whole story. That night, I was exhausted, stressed, and extremely overwhelmed from work. I dosed off behind the wheel. It couldn't have been for more than a minute or two, but when I opened my eyes, I was drifting into oncoming traffic. I cut the wheel hard and got back into my lane just in time, but the terror I felt knowing I could've died was unimaginable. Everything I worked for and accomplished stopped mattering the moment I thought about leaving you and the kids behind."

Laura's eyes widened. "Oh honey, I wish you'd told me." She wrapped her arms around him and gave him a tight hug.

Peter sighed again as he pulled away from her. "I wish I had too. Anyway, a few days after that night, I decided life was too short to waste it not doing what I love. So I've been renting a studio downtown, to sculpt in."

"You've been renting an art studio for nearly a year? Without letting me know?" Laura crossed her arms over her chest. "I know you were trying to cope with what happened. But Peter, you're not alone in all this. You have a family, a wife for God's sake. We could help you if you'd just let us in."

Peter nodded. "I see that now. When I walked off that stage, it was like a weight was lifted off my shoulders. I realized I don't need to hide anymore. I can finally walk in my truth and become the me I fought so long not to become."

Laura sighed, then looked at Peter and said, "I'm still upset about all the lies, but we've got bigger problems on our hands. Like what you're going to do for a living. And what we're going to tell your parents." She gave a small smile. "I'm not looking forward to that call."

"I know. It's not going to be easy," Peter said, reaching to take her hand. "But I also know we'll get through it. Together."

The Masks We Wear: Explanation
Awareness vs. Reactiveness

What are the Mindless Behaviors?
Masks are the personas we create so people in our external environments understand us. A mask, while not representing our true, authentic self, shields us from failures and perceived slights.

Most of us don't know we're wearing a mask because our invented personas please the people around us. Subconsciously, we design them to do this, and when our masks "work," it can lull us into complacency. Peter found his world turned upside down because he'd worn a mask for most of his life without realizing it. He felt so lost and disconnected from his loved ones that he lost his authentic voice.

The unrecognized mask is a dangerous one because of how much energy it takes to maintain, energy which could be focused on your passion and the joys of life. When we unconsciously sacrifice our beliefs and ignore our intuition, our energy reserve is continuously on empty. Work, family, and societal pressures keep us so busy we can't take time to understand the truth we're living.

Most of us are a lot like Peter. We cast ourselves to the wilderness and become lost in identities based on inherited perceptions. Peter operated under the mask of "the politician" because he felt this was his path and the right move for his family and the communities he served.

Masks come with invisible rules that have been implanted for many years, dictating the type of person we should become. Our characters, on the other hand, are unruly and multifaceted, which can at times become exhausting to keep up within social systems that expect us to behave a certain way. The conflict comes from trying to play a role to fit our complex selves into the environments we walk through.

Why do we cling to the Mindless Behaviors?
Awareness puts us in a state of seeing the big picture clearly. Wearing masks, on the other hand, makes us constantly reactive in our settings and awareness. Masks also cause us to make decisions that aren't carefully thought through.

In general, we're unaware of the masks we wear—concern about our reputation, expectations, traditions, societal pressures, relatives, friends, business, and social systems keeps us in a constant state of switching masks from one setting to another. Peter was unaware of the different masks he was wearing. He was living his life on autopilot based on the needs and expectations of his environment.

The masks represent multiple expressions of the persona we embody throughout our life for survival. They are particles of our personality that we put on and take off in different settings. Some of our masks are put upon us because of the situations that are handed to us. Systems limit perceptions, traditions are passed down through time, love comes with conditions, and our inner truths become optional. We're bound to our mundane lives, constantly running on empty with the focus on controlling the narrative of our environment rather than attending to our internal kingdom. These thoughts and perspectives keep us bound to our masks. Peter was stuck between honoring family tradition and following his heart. He thought if he allowed people to uncover his truth, he would be cast out and judged. The idea of letting family, friends, and coworkers down kept him clinging to a reality that wasn't his own. Buried in denial, he wore a mask until it almost took his life.

Peter's mask felt comfortable to him because it was normal based on how the outside world perceived him. But behind closed doors, he clearly battled with it for a long time. Being comfortable feels safe; in most cases, it provides the security of knowing what the next step is. A great example is our daily routine. Peter took a long time to get out of his career until his "normal" became uncomfortable for him. He knew it would be in his best interest to change even though he was walking into the unknown by returning to his art. In many traditions and cultures, the unknown is perceived negatively when compared to sticking to what is known to work.

Our fear is guided by our external environments, which we're forced to please at every moment. Most of the time, it's fear that keeps us in the masks we wear and living in survival mode.

How do we overcome mindlessness?

There are two types of awareness in the journey of getting to know ourselves: internal awareness and situational awareness.

Internal awareness is a sense of knowing who you are in any life situation. Becoming internally aware means being able to be insightful and look within for self-growth in understanding your desires. You can channel your emotions and thoughts to make informed decisions. It also allows you to explore your strengths and weaknesses, which opens the door to self-mastery.

The great power of internal awareness is being comfortable in who you are and how you show up in the world. Since masks represent multiple facets of our character, we can utilize them to better understand ourselves and the environments we live in. Masks are the building blocks to our inner selves, but masks can also harm a person if they don't understand how a mask can affect life situations. Society makes it complicated to grow into our authentic self, but exploring our internal kingdom allows us to feel secure within ourselves no matter what life throws at us.

Situational awareness is understanding the environment you are in—allowing yourself to process what you're feeling, hearing, seeing, and saying. It's important to regularly take stock of the environment we live in—is the company you're keeping challenging you to grow? Or are you simply maintaining the status quo because it's familiar to you?

Learning to be secure in yourself leads to learning to be secure in your environments, which can give you the courage to change your environment as necessary to create the life you want. Peter understood he needed to change so he could be happier and more engaged in his life. His story reflects the struggle we all have with masks from time to time. Once we start to become better communicators within our environments, it can lead to sustainable relationships in the end.

Awareness of his condition started Peter on the path to understanding his identity. He began to come into his true self and slowly started to build a life that worked for him while transitioning out of a life that didn't. Peter stopped clinging to his mask when he realized how it affected him psychically—namely, the loss of time with his family. He was also far removed from the people he loved to serve, communities that barely knew him. While it might have been fulfilling for a while, his work became a cross he couldn't bear. Coming close to death made him realize he'd barely lived, blindly stumbling through life in a mask he couldn't see.

Peter's story illustrates the power of choice versus opportunity. Peter had the opportunity to become a politician, which led to him impacting others' lives. He also had the choice to leave the Senate because he was exhausted and disconnected from his work. Peter had an opportunity to pursue his dream and create the life he truly wanted. Even more, he could still rebuild a connection with his family and make it even stronger. We have the choice to make the right decisions, but we must understand we have one in order to enhance our lives. Once we understand our choices, we can then see the opportunities contained within them.

In the story, Peter mentions that when he was young, he was an artist. As time passed, however, he came to assume he couldn't make a living with art, a decision his family influenced. This shows that as humans connect, we care too much about what's going on in our outside world and don't tap into the person within.

What can we learn from our Mindless Behaviors?
Understanding the nature of your masks is vital for growth, which leads to self-awareness. Becoming aware of our masks helps us become better at making effective decisions that can positively impact the people around us. The essential part is to learn from our masks and integrate their lessons to build the life we dream of without severing our identities. Step back and observe your masks; ask yourself the tough questions on why a mask

is necessary. Then imagine a world where your authentic self is accepted and having a veil is uncomfortable. You're fulfilling your passion, resurrecting your potential, and living your best life.

Self-reflection questions to ask when you encounter masks:

- Am I being my authentic self?

_____

_____

_____

_____

_____

- Is this situation helping me?

_____

_____

_____

_____

_____

Chapter Two

UNREALISTIC EXPECTATIONS

"Good morning, honey! How did you sleep? Do you want some breakfast?" Pamela asked.

"Morning, Mom!" Lisa said. "I slept okay. And sure, I'll have some breakfast." She hugged her mother and slowly walked to the kitchen table with her head down.

Pamela watched her daughter with concern as she put her breakfast in front of her. "Lisa, are you okay?"

"Yes, Mom, I'm fine," Lisa said, though her voice shook. "I just haven't been able to sleep very well lately with everything going on at work."

"Sweetie, you have to take it easy. You've been through a lot," Pamela said.

Lisa heaved a sigh. "Mom, I know you mean well, but I don't need you to tell me what to do. Besides, right now my career is all I have. I have to focus on it."

"I'm know you're an adult, honey, I'm just trying to help. You really do need to take care of yourself," Pamela said.

Lisa rolled her eyes. "Whatever, Mom." She got up

from the kitchen table and kissed her mom on the forehead. "I need to get to work."

An hour later, Lisa was walking into the lobby of People Incorporated. As she did, she gazed at the wall where they showcased staff accomplishments, looking at the various certificates and plaques as if seeing them for the first time. She stopped at one picture—a photo of her and Roger accepting a medal from the mayor—and stared at it for a long time.

After a few minutes, her assistant walked up to her. "Good morning, Lisa! How are you today?" Nancy asked. "Still basking in glory?"

"Glory?" Lisa murmured, still gazing at the picture. "What glory?"

"For the Hero grant, silly!" Nancy said. "If I'd won a $500,000 grant for us, I'd be jumping up and down for weeks. Are you okay?"

"Oh right, the grant," Lisa said, forcing a smile. "I'm fine, I've just got a lot on my mind. Speaking of, do you have that report I asked for?"

"Sure do. I'll go email it right now."

"Thanks," Lisa said before hurrying away to her office. *Boy, the day has barely started and I'm already acting like a space cadet. Got to focus.*

But when Lisa reached her office, she didn't sit down to work right away. Instead, she stared out the window, lost in thought. In her job, she helped different stakeholders and government officials write public policies to benefit underserved communities. Over the years she'd developed a reputation for being a tireless go-getter, someone who made sure each person who crossed her path got the resources they needed. She was also well liked within her professional network, which included many different communities and funding sources, as well as powerful government decision-makers.

Lisa's personal life, however, was anything but amazing. After ten years of marriage, she and her husband, Roger, had divorced six months earlier. Toward the end, they fought over Lisa's job constantly. Each time she accepted a new project or volunteered to spearhead a new initiative, Roger got angrier and Lisa got more defensive, even though privately she agreed with him—her personal life was slipping away. With Roger now out of the picture, Lisa threw herself into work even more, often staying at the office late into the night.

Just then the phone rang, interrupting her ruminations.

"Hello, this is Lisa Gavin speaking."

"Lisa, hello! It's Clint Jackson. We used to work together at the Regis Foundation, remember?"

"Clint!" Lisa exclaimed. "Of course I remember you. What a nice surprise. How have you been? Last I heard, you were still at Creed."

"That's actually why I'm calling," he said. "I put in my notice a couple months ago. I've started a new nonprofit. It's called Roots, and our focus is on offering resources to people in underrepresented communities to help them thrive in the workforce. I'm putting a team together, and of course I thought of you. Would you be interested in being our executive director? You would be running all day-to-day operations, and you'd be able to pick your own team."

"What? But why me?" Lisa said.

"Well, we're looking for a candidate with strong community ties and a history of securing big grants, so naturally I thought of you," Clint replied. "What do you say?"

Lisa sat in stunned silence. This was the opportunity of a lifetime. As executive director, she would still have to answer to a board, but she would have authority over an entire organization. Still, she was hesitant—the divorce had left her exhausted and wondering if she should take time away from her career to focus on fixing the shambles of her personal life. But could she really let this job slip through her fingers?

After a few moments, Lisa found her voice again. "That is an amazing offer, Clint, and very flattering. Can I have a few days to think it over?"

Clint laughed. "Same old Lisa, always thinking through the pros and cons. Of course, take all the time you need."

Days passed as Lisa pondered her decision. More than once she wished Roger were still there; he was always good at helping her work through hard choices. But the love of her life was gone, and for the first time in over a decade, Lisa had to make a big decision on her own.

Eventually, she called Clint back. "I'd love to take the position," she said.

"That's wonderful! Out of curiosity, what made you decide to go for it?"

Lisa laughed ruefully. "To be honest, my personal life is a bit of a wreck right now. I could really use a goal that's clear and achievable, and I can't think of a better one than helping Roots get off the ground."

"Understood," said Clint. "Well, whatever the reason, I'm thrilled to have you on board. See you on Monday."

———

Over the following months, Lisa threw herself into her new role. The more she worked, the less time she had to deal with the emotional fallout from her divorce and her increasing detachment from her family and friends.

One of Lisa's first major tasks at Roots was hiring full-time staffers. After perusing hundreds of applications and conducting endless rounds of interviews, Lisa eventually hired eight people. Her first hire was a woman named Morgan, who was joining the organization as an office and project manager. With her wealth of office management experience, Morgan quickly became Lisa's right hand. All the other employees reported to Morgan, and she was also in charge of daily operations whenever Lisa was traveling.

This arrangement worked well for everyone for several months. But as time passed and Lisa's travel schedule ramped up, she and Morgan communicated less and less. Their near-daily phone check-ins turned into biweekly touch-bases, which Lisa often canceled or put off. She would also take days to respond to emails, even ones about important matters like budgets or strategic planning.

Morgan, who couldn't move forward without Lisa's approval, increasingly found her hands tied at work. She began to dread Lisa's returns to the office, which always played out the same way: Lisa would sweep into the office shouting at no one in particular, "Didn't you guys get *anything* done while I was out?" Then Morgan would quietly explain the staff couldn't work if Lisa didn't give them direction, to which Lisa would usually respond, "Excuses, excuses, excuses." Lisa started to get a reputation for withholding information from the staff and putting off projects until the last minute. This not only caused mass miscommunication but also forced staffers to work overtime to hit deadlines.

Rather than give her team more notice or clearer

deadlines, Lisa reprimanded Morgan for allowing them to work overtime. After a while, Lisa stopped approving overtime altogether, demoralizing her staff and stoking a buildup of animosity aimed squarely at her.

One day, she stormed up to Morgan's desk. "Lionel at the Thrive Foundation just called to ask why we missed their grant application deadline. How could you drop the ball on that?"

"What do you mean?" asked Morgan. "I've been calling and emailing you about it for months, and I sent you the application draft to review two weeks ago. Didn't you see it?"

"Morgan, there's no way you sent me that grant. If you had, I would've reviewed and submitted it."

"But I did, I swear!" Morgan said. "I even scheduled a meeting on your calendar to review it." She paused, then began again slowly, as if choosing her words carefully. "Our communication has been . . . sparse over the last few months. To be honest, I'm surprised this is the first time something's slipped through the cracks. Without your approval, it's nearly impossible to—"

Lisa cut her off. "So you're saying this is my fault."

"No, not at all, I just—"

"I don't want to have this conversation out here in front of everyone," said Lisa. Before Morgan could answer, Lisa turned on her heel and stomped away to her office. Morgan snatched up her laptop and followed.

Inside Lisa's office, Morgan quickly pulled up a list of all the emails she'd sent to Lisa about the Thrive grant. "Lisa, please look at this," she said, pointing to the screen. "I'm not blaming you, but I document everything we do in this office, and as you can see, I sent you several emails about Thrive." She closed the laptop lid, then looked Lisa in the eye. "I can't run an office if you won't give me the information I need to be successful. How can we get on the same page?"

"I gave you as much information as you needed to get the job done!" Lisa snapped. "I think the real problem here is that you don't know what you're doing. For one thing, you have employees working overtime for no apparent reason. How do I know they're not submitting false hours?"

"What?" Morgan exclaimed. "How would you know when you're barely in this office? And when you do come in, all you do is bark orders at us!" She leaned back in her seat and tried to calm herself. "Lisa, you're the face of this organization and our leader. If you don't talk to me or give us sustainable directives, how are we supposed to be successful?"

Lisa was silent for a moment. Then she said, "Well, part of your job is supposed to be keeping me on track and making the office run as smoothly as possible. Clearly, dropping the ball on the Thrive grant signals a big problem." She turned to stare out her office window. "You know what, Morgan? I don't think this is working out. You can pack your things and leave. You're released from your duties."

Morgan sat in shock, her jaw hanging open and her eyes wide. But she didn't fight Lisa's decision. In tears, she stormed out of Lisa's office and began cleaning out her desk. Within thirty minutes, she was gone.

A few minutes later, Lisa emerged from her office.

"After some deep thought and discussion with the board, I regret to announce that Morgan no longer works in this office," she said. "We'll be announcing the search for a new operations director in the coming weeks." Without further explanation, she returned to her office and shut the door with an audible click.

The employees were shocked. They started whispering among themselves, confused about what had just happened. The thought of Morgan not being there terrified them, because it meant only one thing: Lisa would be around a lot more.

Over the next few months, the environment at Roots grew extremely toxic. Communication was still limited;

the weekly project status email became monthly, then stopped completely. Lisa only came out of her office on the rare days a board member stopped by, and even then, she usually whisked them away to lunch before they could say a word to the staff. One by one, employees left the organization until there were only two left besides Lisa.

Word travels fast in the nonprofit community. Everyone soon knew about the problems at Roots, which made it hard for Lisa to find new employees. The organization that had once had multiple people competing for job openings was now a place no one wanted to work at. The board grew suspicious and began asking probing questions. When a group of former Roots employees filed a lawsuit for wage theft and the case hit the news, Clint called Lisa.

"Hello, Lisa, how are you doing?"

"I'm okay," Lisa responded. "I take it you've seen the news."

"Yes. Obviously, we have to address these allegations. The board just called an emergency meeting at 10:00 a.m. It's mandatory that you attend."

"Ten? But it's already 8:00 a.m. now," Lisa said.

"I know," Clint snapped. "We'll be there in a couple of hours. I would cancel all your meetings for the day." He hung up before Lisa could respond.

Lisa quickly got dressed and hopped in the car. On her way to the meeting, she worried about what the board members would say. *I can't afford to lose this position,* she thought to herself. When she finally made it to the office, she sat in her car for thirty minutes thinking about how she was going to explain what had transpired over the past few months. *How did I get here?* she wondered. Then, *Breathe, Lisa!*

Lisa walked into the conference room at ten o'clock on the dot. Clint and all twelve of the other board members were already there. Leon, the board chair, asked Lisa to have a seat.

"Lisa, the reason for this meeting is to talk about your conduct and the complaints we've been receiving from former employees," Leon intoned. "Can you tell us what's been going on?"

"Well," she said, trying to steady her voice, "it's been a struggle to keep up with the workload and manage the team. I was under the impression the people I hired were qualified to successfully fulfill their roles. But to my disappointment, they were constantly late turning in their projects. With all my travel, I couldn't micromanage every detail. I trusted that my team could keep the organization running smoothly while I was away. Unfortunately, it looks like that trust was misplaced."

She scanned the board members for any reactions,

but their stony faces revealed nothing. An awkward silence hung over the room for several moments.

"Thank you for that explanation," Leon finally said. "It seems like your previous team has a different perspective on what happened, especially Morgan, your project manager. She forwarded multiple emails between the two of you, which we all reviewed before this meeting. Based on those emails and other communications with your team, we believe you withheld important information that prevented them from completing their work effectively. Missing the Thrive grant deadline appears to be only one negative incident among many."

"Wait, I can explain—" Lisa responded.

"Let me finish," Leon said, cutting her off. "Lisa, we trusted you to lead Roots because of all your past successes. We admire all the great community-building work you've done, but something tells me there's more to this story than you're letting on." He shook his head. "I've watched you through the years, and this all just seems completely out of character."

Lisa was quiet for a couple of minutes. Then she came clean about what was really going on: the dismal morale, the forced overtime, the screaming matches. In response, the board put Lisa on a three-month leave of absence, "to give you time to reflect." The decision hurt her immeasurably, but she understood their reasoning—how could they trust her to fix Roots's problems now?

Lisa knew three months away from her job would feel like an eternity. Work had become her life—she couldn't function without it. But the time had come for her to face herself and the decisions she'd made.

As Lisa was leaving the meeting and heading to her car, her cell phone rang. She looked at the screen: it was her mother. Though she didn't feel like talking, she decided to answer anyway.

"Hi, Mom. How are you?"

"I'm fine, honey. What's going on? I saw you and your organization on the news. Are you okay?" Lisa could hear the deep concern in her voice.

"No, Mom, I'm not okay. The board just put me on a three-month leave of absence. I don't know what's going to happen to my job. It's all pretty uncertain at this point."

"Oh honey, I'm so sorry. I know how much that job meant to you," her mother cooed into the phone. "But you know, I think this could be a good thing, Lisa. With everything that's happened in the last year, you could use a break. Focus on yourself till you can get a handle on things."

Lisa began to cry quietly. "Oh, Mom, how did I get here?" she asked. "When I started at Roots, everything seemed so promising and exciting. What did I do wrong?"

"Sweetie, you got here because you didn't give yourself time to heal from the divorce. After you and Roger split up, you got so wrapped up in your work that you abandoned your personal life. I barely see you, and it seems like you don't even talk to your friend Brooke anymore. You know, she called me just the other day to ask about you. She said she'd called you multiple times but never heard back."

Lisa cringed. "I know, I just haven't had time to call her. I've been so wrapped up in work. I thought that was what I needed," she said. "I was so lonely after the divorce . . . work seemed like the perfect way to get my sense of self back. But now, I feel less like myself than ever. I don't even know who I am without Roots."

"Lisa, breathe. You don't have to figure everything out this minute," her mother said. "Start by taking things one day at a time. And come over! I don't want you staying in that big drafty house alone tonight."

Lisa smiled through her tears. "Okay, Mom, I'll be there in an hour."

Setting Unrealistic Expectations: Explanation

Living to Work vs. Working to Live

What are the Mindless Behaviors?
We spend most of our lives building our professional careers and climbing society's different ladders. Many times, our work is so much the focus of our lives that we forget to do the self-care necessary to maintain the other areas.

Lisa abandoned her personal life to pursue her dream job. Each time she rose in her career and more responsibilities were placed on her shoulders, she missed opportunities to put personal boundaries in place around her time and energy. She simply continued working as hard as possible, driving her personal life even further into the background. Even though she clearly needed support, she often rejected offers of help from her friends and family because deep down she believed she didn't need anyone.

Lisa's work/life imbalance put a strain on her team, which led to missed deadlines and other workplace inefficiencies. She created an authoritarian environment with no sense of collaboration, striking fear in her employees for even asking the necessary questions to get their work done. In sum, Lisa wore the world on her shoulders, bearing the constant feeling she alone had to do everything.

Lisa made her work a priority because success in this area seemed achievable. As she climbed the career ladder, it made her feel proud and secure to persevere within a realm she understood (unlike the unpredictable landscape of her failed marriage). Lisa's scarcity mindset also affected her decisions; in part, she took the position with Roots because she believed a bigger one might never come.

When something isn't going right, often the first thing we want to do is mask the pain. But while indulging in distractions like work might help you avoid pain for a little while, it rarely works in the long run. As Lisa realized when she talked with her mom, only taking a break from her work world to confront her inner demons would bring her lasting peace.

Why do we cling to the Mindless Behaviors?
We spread ourselves thin because of the constant battle between living to work and working to live. Living to work means putting your career first while pushing your personal life into the background, while working to live means considering work as simply a means to an end, the end being a lifestyle that aligns with your passions and interests.

When we're working to live, we cling to the idea that we have to put work before having a social life. This mindset usually starts in school, where the focus is on educating individuals with the hope that knowledge will help them find a good job someday. Later, self-help books, career advice websites, and our peers and family members remind us that the only way to get ahead in life is to work on our careers. Thus firmly defined by our jobs and career prospects, we take on any and all responsibilities placed on us, even when they don't fit into our workload.

At the heart of this behavior, we find a sense of pride in our need to control the outside world and a deep-seated desire for perfection. These actions, while harmful to our personal growth, are often praised in modern life: pride becomes "self-confidence," a need for control is viewed as "leadership ability," and perfectionism transforms into "high standards" when viewed through the lens of unrealistic expectations. This makes it all the harder to let go of the mindless behavior: If people are praising us, why should we change our ways?

Lisa had another reason to cling to the mindless behavior of unrealistic expectations: her impressive track record. Lisa showed over the course of her career before Roots that she could make an impact on her community through dedication and hard work. As an inflated sense of her accomplishments set in, Lisa became unreasonable, believing her stellar record justified her toxic behavior at work. Compounding the problem was that Lisa's reputation acted as a shield for quite some time, allowing her to get away with things people generally wouldn't be able to when starting a new job.

How do we overcome mindlessness?

Unrealistic expectations require gaining a deeper understanding of your limitations and becoming a more vocal advocate for your personal growth and well-being. Our reactive world is filled with busyness; if we don't understand that this is a moment in time, we'll start to get lost in our own lives.

Lisa's story sheds additional light on how leadership can challenge us and how managers can create toxic environments they're unaware of. Most of the time, the higher you are in a job hierarchy, the more responsibilities you take on, which can lead to overload and ultimately a lack of balance. For leaders, it's important to balance taking on responsibilities with delegating work (and control) to our teams and employees whenever possible.

Growth begins with acknowledging our shortcomings and holding ourselves accountable for our actions. Throughout the story, Lisa made major mistakes and blamed her staff for them. She covered up the situation with the board due to her inability to face the toxic environment she had created.

When we make mistakes, it's often hard to admit it, especially if our actions affected other people. It's easier to blame subordinate or external factors than to dig into what we did wrong. But when you don't take responsibility for your actions (as was the case with Lisa), you lose the respect of the environments you live in. Conversely, when we walk in the path of accountability, it's easy for people to see themselves assisting us in achieving our goals.

Communication, with ourselves and others, is key to establishing balance in our lives. Lisa was unaware of the lack of communication inside herself. At every step of her story she ignored the pain and loneliness she felt, subconscious communication from her intuition. Once she came into the position and started overseeing multiple people, the situation got even worse. Now Lisa's communication barriers weren't just harming her own well-being, they were also keeping her team in the dark. Becoming aware of how we communicate internally and externally can lead to healthier outcomes.

Seeking advice from family and friends and allowing them to assist you also provides an opportunity to overcome obstacles. Lisa didn't feel she had the appropriate support network to rely on when she needed it most, so she became the person everyone leaned on for answers. As a result, she kept her own problems to herself, wrongly believing no one could help her. If she'd instead been open and humble in seeking advice, she might have gained insights about solving the problems in her workplace. Our support networks can influence how we show up in our life; being open to another person's perspective will guide you in many ways.

What can we learn from our Mindless Behaviors?
Our external world has so many expectations for us that we often get pulled in multiple directions without centering our mind and self. We can easily place limits on what we do personally ("I'm going to eat less candy," for example). But setting boundaries in our careers is a bigger challenge because we trade our time and energy for money, even though we usually can't control the product or output that results from that time.

It's important to stop clinging to unrealistic expectations. Your personal life will most likely affect your career when it is unaligned, so prioritize your life in a way that will bring you the best results and create boundaries around what you can handle and what you can't. Being comfortable walking away from an opportunity, even if it looks good on paper, is sometimes the best thing you can do to support your well-being.

Self-reflection questions to ask when you encounter unrealistic expectations:

- Is this the right opportunity for me?

_____

_____

_____

- What value will I get from this opportunity?

- How might this opportunity serve my higher purpose?

Chapter Three

ENABLING BAD BEHAVIOR

Bianca was sitting in rush hour traffic when her cell phone rang. "Hey, Tasha, what's going on?" she said.

"Nothing, girl! Are you off work yet? We're having drinks at Blue Mirage and we really want to see you."

"I don't know," said Bianca. "I'm tired. It's been a crazy couple of weeks."

"All the more reason to treat yourself to some drinks! Come on, it's not the same without you here," Tasha pleaded.

Bianca sighed. "Who all is there?"

"You know, the usual," Tasha chirped. "Me, Renee, Marie . . ."

"Is Carlos there?"

"No, of course not! I wouldn't be calling you if he was."

After a long pause, Bianca finally gave in. "Okay," she said. "I'll stop by for a little while. But I can't stay out too late and—"

"Great, see you soon!" Tasha hung up before Bianca could answer.

On the drive to the restaurant, Bianca went back and forth in her mind, debating whether to go or not. Normally, she loved meeting her friends for happy hour, but today she was utterly exhausted. With everything that had happened in the last few weeks—her night classes, an important new project, sick family members—she would've rather stayed home than go out for a girls' night. *Just one drink,* she promised herself; then her stomach growled loudly. *Okay, one drink and an appetizer. Then straight home to bed.*

As she drove, she willed herself to think positively. She hadn't seen Renee, Marie, or Tasha for a couple of weeks, so this would be an excellent time to catch up. She pulled up, parked the car, and walked into the restaurant, a smile growing on her face. With a newfound energy, Bianca was ready to take the night by storm.

As she walked in, her phone buzzed with an incoming text from Tasha: "We're done eating and about to go, where R U?????"

Bianca nearly dropped her phone. *Leaving? I can't be that late, can I?* Before she could frantically text Tasha to wait, she nearly knocked her over in the restaurant lobby.

"Oh my god, Bianca, you're here! We thought you were standing us up *again.* Renee and Marie are in the bathroom. I can't believe how long it's been since I've seen you!" Before Bianca could answer, Tasha pulled her into a tight hug, then leaned away to hold her at arm's length. "Look, I should just tell you right now: we're going to Carlos's place, and you're coming with us."

"What?" Bianca said, much louder than she'd meant to. A server gave her a dirty look and she lowered her voice. "And why do we all need to go my ex's house, exactly?"

"His brother Rodney's moving to Florida for a job, so Carlos decided to throw him a party," Tasha said. "It'll be fun!"

"Oh yeah," Bianca murmured. "Carlos said something about that a few weeks ago. I totally forgot."

Tasha's eyes widened. "You mean you two have been *talking*? Do tell!"

"It's not like that," Bianca said with a sigh. "My mom told me his aunt Laura died last month, so I reached out. They were close, so I figured he'd be having a hard time. Just because we're not dating anymore doesn't mean I don't care about him."

Tasha smirked. "Whatever you say," she said. "Well, I guess this just means you're definitely coming to the party then. You wouldn't want to leave poor Carlos alone in his time of need." She laughed as she turned to wave at Renee and Marie, who'd just turned up. "And besides, you have to give us a ride," Tasha said.

"What happened to Jimmy?" Bianca asked. Tasha's

husband loved chauffeuring her and her friends around; it gave him a chance to show off his latest SUV.

"He's away all week on business," she said. "Come on, Bee, please?"

"I don't know," said Bianca, wavering. "Texting about his aunt is one thing. Going to a party at his house is another. I just don't think it's a good idea."

"You'll be fine," Renee said. "We'll make sure you have so much fun you won't even notice Carlos."

Tasha and Marie nodded their agreement. Still, a single thought flashed through Bianca's mind: *It's a trap!* Ever since their breakup four years earlier, her friends had been on a relentless mission to reunite her and Carlos. It was like a pet hobby or science experiment for them. Even though Bianca had told them numerous times she and Carlos were happier apart, they never let up, constantly updating her about his latest girlfriend or comparing every man she dated to him, always unfavorably.

"Look," Bianca said as the women walked to her car, "Carlos and I will always have a connection. But we couldn't see eye to eye on enough things to make it work. Plus, we all know it was only a matter of time before he got bored and started messing with other women—that's been his MO practically since we were kids." She shook her head, recalling the legions of girls in their middle school who'd had a crush on Carlos, who had been only too happy to flirt with them all. "I don't need that drama in my life."

Renee sat in the front passenger seat and pulled on her seatbelt. "Bee, whatever happens, we're with you. But nothing is going to happen, so relax."

Bianca glanced over, frowning. "I wasn't even really invited, you know. He probably only brought the party up by accident. And isn't he still dating that woman?" She put the car in gear and set out on the short drive to Carlos's, ashamed at how easily the directions came back to her, as if she still drove to his place every day.

"Ugh, Rachel. Carlos is so wrong for that," Renee said. "He shouldn't string you two along! I don't care if he's my cousin, it's just wrong."

"Renee, for the last time, we're not together! Carlos can do whatever he wants and date whomever he wants. He's a grown man."

"So you're saying you don't have any feelings for him, not even the tiniest bit?" Marie piped up from the back seat. "I mean, I know you guys broke up a while ago, but you were practically engaged! Doesn't that mean anything?"

Bianca stared out the window. It was true, texting with Carlos about his aunt hadn't been all sad. The conversation had quickly fallen into their old pattern: his wry jokes, her snarky responses, their ability to finish each other's thoughts.

She met Marie's eyes in the rearview mirror. "I guess it wouldn't be the worst thing to see him. And who knows, maybe I do need to get clear on what we are to each other now. We never really sat down and had a heart-to-heart when we broke up. It just sort of . . . ended." Bianca stared out the window again, watching other cars speed past. "Maybe we do need to talk."

"Yes!" said Tasha.

"Finally, you're getting it!" Marie added.

"You're so right, Bee," Tasha said, reaching forward to pat Bianca's shoulder. "This'll be good for both of you."

Bianca gave a thin, half-hearted smile. "I hope so, Tee. I really hope so."

———

Bianca's determination to talk to Carlos vanished as soon as they parked in front of his house. *What am I doing?* she thought. *This isn't me. Not even close.*

She looked over at her friends, who were adjusting their outfits and makeup. "I don't want to go in," she said.

"Bianca, you're fine," said Tasha. "You belong here as much as any of us. Let's go!"

"Okay," said Bianca. She gathered herself and walked to Carlos's front door—it looked exactly the same as when she'd slammed it on her way out four years earlier, suitcase in hand, never to return again, or so she'd thought. Her heart was pounding, and a wave of gut-churning anxiety washed over her.

She raised her hand to knock but couldn't do it. After a moment Tasha pushed past her and pressed the doorbell, hard. "Geez, Bee, snap out of it."

Ben, Carlos's roommate, opened the door. "Welcome, everyone!" He did a double take when he saw Bianca but managed to cover it with a smile. Mostly. "Hi, Bee," he said. "Long time no see. I didn't know you were coming."

"Hey, Ben. Yeah, I didn't know I was coming either until about fifteen minutes ago." Bianca felt as if she were dying a thousand deaths under Ben's curious stare. It was as if all the wind had been knocked out of her and she didn't know how to get it back.

"Well, welcome anyway." He stepped aside to let the women pass. "Food's in the kitchen, drinks are down in the basement."

Renee, Marie, and Tasha glanced over at her, conspiratorial smiles on their faces. *Do they think this is funny?* Bianca wondered. She certainly didn't; the thought of walking into that house felt like falling down a dark hole with no exit. *Pull yourself together, Bianca!* she chided herself. *You've already shown up at your ex's party with no invite. At least things can't get any worse.*

Once inside, Tasha and Renee quickly disappeared into the crowd of partygoers crammed into the kitchen. Marie and Bianca went into the living room and found a free spot on the couch.

"Are you okay?" Marie asked. "You looked like you saw a ghost when Ben opened the door."

"No, I'm not okay," Bianca said. "To be honest, it feels really weird to be here. Weird and uncomfortable."

Marie patted her hand. "You just need to relax, that's all. Let's go get you a drink."

Before Bianca could protest about having to drive, Marie was pulling her down the basement stairs. Once they'd threaded their way through the crowd in front of the drinks table, she quickly poured a large shot of vodka into a plastic cup. She pushed it into Bianca's hand. "Come on, drink up!"

"Who's going to drive us all home?" Bianca said.

"Lyft. Uber," Marie said. She rolled her eyes. "Jesus, Bee, it's just one drink."

Bianca sighed. "You're not going to let this go, are you?"

"Not a chance," Marie said. "Now take your medicine— doctor's orders!"

Against her better judgement, Bianca downed the vodka in one long swallow. Within minutes she could feel the warmth from the alcohol flowing through her body. Slowly her shoulders relaxed as she eased into aimless small talk with Marie—*Maybe this wasn't such a bad idea after all,* she thought.

Suddenly a deep male voice boomed from the stairs. "Hey, this where the party went?"

Bianca turned toward the staircase, though she didn't have to—she knew it was Carlos. Still, when he reached the basement and she saw his face, the bottom fell out of her stomach.

It was as if Carlos felt Bianca looking at him. He locked eyes with her from across the room, but Bianca couldn't read his expression in the dim basement light—confused? angry? mocking?

"There she is!" Tasha's scream pierced through the party noise. Bianca hadn't noticed her and Renee trailing Carlos down the stairs. They shouldered their way past partygoers, Carlos in tow.

When they reached Bianca and Marie, Carlos had a shocked expression on his face. "Bianca, hi. Tasha and Renee told me you were here, but I didn't believe it."

Bianca's cheeks burned. "They asked me for a ride. I didn't want to come. I mean, not that I didn't want to be here, I mean—"

"It's great that you came," Carlos interrupted. "I just know parties weren't your thing back when . . . we were together."

Just then, a woman walked over to Carlos and wrapped her arm around his waist. "Carlos, honey, we're running really low on ice. Can I take your car to grab more? Mine's blocked in." The way she looked at him as she spoke, as if they were the only two people in the room, instantly told Bianca they were together.

"Sure." Carlos reached for his pocket, then seemed to think better of it. "Actually, uh, I think I left my keys in the kitchen. I'll go grab them." He reached for the woman's arm and pulled her toward the stairs.

"You don't have to come," she protested. "Stay and talk to your friends."

"They're fine," he muttered. Then the pair were out of earshot, swallowed up by the crowd.

Marie stood in silence. Inside, Bianca was cringing. *Oh my god, that was so awkward!* And it was clear Carlos had been equally uncomfortable. He was probably telling his new girlfriend right now about his ex who just showed up at his party uninvited.

Renee and Tasha, who'd watched with wide eyes while Carlos and Bianca talked, suddenly came to life. They hugged her from either side, cooing in her ears.

"Oh god, Bee!"

"That must've been so embarrassing."

"I can't believe the way she was all over him, right in front of you!"

"And he just stood there eating it up."

"But we're here for you, sweetie. No matter what."

Underneath their flurry of soothing words, Bianca heard something else—amusement. *Are they seriously getting a laugh out of this?* she wondered. *Not funny!*

"Bee," Tasha said, squeezing her hand, "you want a glass of wine?"

Bianca felt exhausted and small under Tasha and Renee's onslaught. "Sure, whatever. Pour me a glass. Red."

Tasha laughed. "That's my girl!"

Bianca spent the next hour hovering by the drinks table, clutching her wine without drinking it. Through it all, Marie lectured Bianca about how she should never have texted Carlos about his aunt, and that coming to his house had been an even bigger mistake.

"Your and Carlos's time has passed," she said. "There's a lesson in all this, Bee, and it's up to you to figure it out. *I* think that to move forward, you have to cut ties with his family, or else this'll just be a vicious cycle of . . . *codependency*." Marie sounded out the word carefully, as if she were repeating someone else's words.

Bianca rolled her eyes, but Marie was too distracted to notice. *God, someone's been watching too much Oprah.*

Tasha and Renee flitted in and out, giving regular reports on Carlos's whereabouts. He was apparently holed up in a corner of the backyard. Bianca couldn't help thinking he was avoiding the house because of her, as if her mere presence had tainted it.

Eventually the dam inside her burst. "Sorry, I've got to get some air," she blurted out. Before her friends could stop her, she'd raced up the stairs and out of the house. She ran to her car, jumped inside, and sped away toward home as quickly as she could.

As she drove to her apartment, tears flowed down her face. She felt so stupid—how had she gotten into this predicament?

Just then, while she was sitting at a stoplight, Bianca got a text. It was her father. A pastor, he often sent her random Bible verses for comfort, "and to get you thinking," as he liked to say. This one read, "Today you shall part with every inherited garment of disappointment, frustration, shame, untimely death, disgrace, failure, sickness, and disease that invades you at the brink of your miracles. Isaiah 43:18–19."

After reading the verse, Bianca fell into deep reflection. She thought about the pain she felt over how she'd handled her friends and Carlos. *I have to figure out why I constantly let people walk all over me,* she realized. As the light turned green, Bianca steered with one hand and wiped away her tears with the other. *It's time to stop crying and start asking myself some tough questions.*

Enabling Bad Behaviors: Explanation

Giving Your Power Away vs. Standing in Your Power

What are the Mindless Behaviors?

In our external environments, we're often pressured to do things we're uncomfortable with because of the people around us. Bianca allowed her friends to put her in an uncomfortable situation even though she knew it would be detrimental to her well-being. She became a passenger in the situation and gave her friends the wheel, allowing them to control the outcome.

Sometimes we're too close to friends and family members to consider their words and actions objectively. This was one of Bianca's problems—she didn't follow her intuition due to blind loyalty to her friends.

Another thing that happens when it comes to our loved ones is that we tend to assume we have the answers to their problems but fail to fully acknowledge the pain they're experiencing. Bianca's friends couldn't understand they were leading her into a place that, in the end, could cause her more pain because they were convinced they knew what was best for her. Also, Bianca failed to express her feelings strongly. While she voiced some concerns about going to Carlos's house, her friends took the decision from her due to her inability to stand up for herself.

Close family and friends have a special place in our hearts. When we're around them, our trust and expectations are high, so much so that we share information about ourselves we wouldn't normally share with the outside world. Bianca's frustration stemmed from having multiple encounters with the same close friends that led to the same outcome: drama and heartache. She ignored many red flags along the way, which led to her breakdown toward the end of the story. Like Bianca, we often dismiss information that could be pertinent to our growth when it concerns individuals we're close to.

Why do we cling to the Mindless Behaviors?
We enable bad behaviors because of the battle between giving our power away versus standing in our power.

When you give your power away, you give up control over your life. Operating from a position of scarcity and fear, you allow the external world to make decisions for you, even if they go against your values. Bianca's story illustrates just how much power we can give to environments that don't serve our greater good. Conversely, standing in your power comes from within; you only take in advice and actions that align with the values you hold dear.

The world teaches us how untrusting and unreliable relationships can be. We're regularly bombarded with news about betrayals, broken marriages, abuse, heinous crimes, and unethical practices. We see this in history books and in the world we inhabit today. The elderly, the young, the wise, the lost, the displaced—all play a part in enabling lousy behavior that often starts with a little seed.

The social aspect of our world is in crisis—this is the real reason we constantly give our power away. Everyone's guard is up due to the conditions we're subjected to. In this environment, time becomes the main measure of a fulfilling relationship, leading us to maintain ties even when the relationship is toxic.

The difficult thing about relationships developed over time is that it's challenging to change toxic behavior patterns within them. Most people will put up with bad behavior before risking the loss of a friend or relative. Outside of our close social circles, we must put on our survival hats to navigate life; for this reason, we don't want to engage in other ways of thinking and living. Even though we have the power to change the environments we live in, we ignore our problems instead of finding positive solutions. It's just too much energy to cast a critical eye on the world *and* the company we keep.

Luckily, with time and self-awareness, we can learn to understand how our environments work and focus on relationships that are deeper in value.

How do we overcome mindlessness?

Fully understanding the environment we live in can allow us to come into our power in a healthy and productive way. In Bianca's case, her inability to understand her friends and the role they played in her life on a deeper level promoted a circle of hurt and mistrust.

When we observe our relationships from multiple perspectives, we gain more clarity about them. But it starts with being honest with ourselves. When you find yourself in a bad situation, it's important to do some reflective thinking. Ask yourself, "How did this situation happen, what role did I play in it, and what can I do differently moving forward?"

We mirror the environments we live in; Bianca's behavior around her friends is an example of this. We don't want to lose anything remotely close to us, so much so that we often stay in relationships—whether with spouses, partners, or friends—that go against our beliefs. Luckily, Bianca eventually realized there was an unhealthy cycle perpetuating itself in her friendships with Tasha, Renee, and Marie, one she needed to break.

We humans often don't want to believe our close social circles can mirror the unpredictable world we live in. We think there's a level of security and certainty that comes with having those bonds, and we trust unthinkingly.

Honesty is the primary tool to create lasting

relationships that are impactful and meaningful. But in relationships, we're prone to telling our friends what they want to hear instead of the truth. Bianca's friends knew she wasn't invited to Carlos's party, but they wanted to stir up drama for their own entertainment, so they weren't honest about their true opinions. Bianca wasn't honest with herself about how her friends weren't living up to her expectations of friendship.

We thrive in settings where we have clarity about our relationships and environment. It was clear the communication between Bianca and her friends was broken. She didn't clearly articulate how she felt and why she was reluctant to go to her ex's house. The combination of allowing a series of events to unfold over time along with the latest incident illustrated in this story led Bianca to question herself. She became insightful about how she showed up in the world and how she was perceived within it. This insight set her on the path to understanding her role in the situation and what she needed to do to overcome it.

What can we learn from our Mindless Behaviors?
Bianca's story teaches us the importance of standing in your power. When you give a person or issue permission to make decisions on your behalf, they can do whatever

they want to you. Trusting ourselves more allows us to make better decisions on our own behalf.

One thing we can do is work to understand the role we play in each of our relationships. It's easy to cast judgment on others, saying, "That person is toxic," and pushing them away. But if you're a willing participant in the behavior, you're part of the toxicity. Think through the problem to uncover the unconscious patterns at work behind other people's behaviors and your own.

When it comes to making important decisions about our lives, we must get to the point where we're acting for our benefit and not for others. The environments we live in mirror how we see ourselves, and all relationships are a two-way street; change won't happen unless you're engaged. You should put any tough situation you encounter under observation, examining it from multiple angles.

Self-reflection questions to ask when you encounter bad behaviors:

• What are the specific elements of this situation that are making me feel disposable, unappreciated, or ignored?

_____

_____

- Are my friends truly friends?

- What do I know about my friends beyond surface-level facts?

Chapter Four

NOT FOLLOWING YOUR INTUITION

Eighteen-year-old Ola had just graduated from high school and was now ready to take college by storm. Ola's parents were so proud when they found out their baby boy had chosen biology as a major—they'd always dreamed of having a doctor in the family. Ola was happy his parents were pleased, but deep down, a tiny voice called him to a different direction. But he ignored it, packed his bags, and headed to college, eager to embrace adulthood and his newfound freedom.

For money, Ola built and fixed computers for his friends and family, which had been his hobby for many years. Skilled in building systems from the ground up, he quickly built a reputation as a tech guru. Ola's eyes lit up whenever he worked on computers. His siblings and friends were shocked when he said he was going to school for biology and not computer science.

Once the first semester started, Ola began to question his decision to become a biology major. The subject didn't come naturally to him. No matter how hard he studied or how much extra help he got from his professors, he couldn't retain the information. But despite the difficulties, Ola didn't want to disappoint his parents, so he stuck with the major, determined to improve his grades.

Before proceeding, he decided to chat with his parents about his struggles in school. Ola's father, Peter, gave him a long lecture about staying in biology and assured him that being a doctor was the best route to take. "College is an adjustment," he said. "It'll get better with time. You'll see."

After the conversation, Ola started the second semester determined to stay in biology. At first, it was going well; he seemed to be adjusting to his studies and the energy of college. Then the old anxious feelings came sneaking back in. Feeling confused and disinterested, Ola started to skip his biology classes to work on computers. As time passed, his grades began to slip. Ola was at the point of wanting to drop out of school, and he dreaded the conversation with his parents.

One night, Ola got back to his dorm room and threw himself on his bed facedown. "Man, what a stressful day!" he said to his roommate, Chris.

"I feel you," said Chris. "Yo, a letter came for you. I put it on your desk."

"Thanks. I'll look at it later. Right now, I'm going to

hit the shower and unwind. I can't focus. These science courses are hard as hell," Ola responded.

"You ever thought about changing your major?" Chris asked. "You're good with computers. Every time I see you you're working on someone's device."

"Nah, that's just a hobby," Ola said.

"Well, you should think about it."

Ola left to hit the showers. Later, he decided to open the letter. Within minutes, the relaxing end-of-day moments became gut-wrenching and stressful as Ola read the words *Unsatisfactory. Probation. Threat of expulsion.* Tears came to his eyes as he bowed his head in shame, wondering what he would tell his parents. *How did I get here?* he asked himself. *What's wrong with me?*

Ola took a walk to call his older sister, Esther. For the past several months, he'd been talking to her about his experiences in college off and on.

"Hello?"

"Hi, Esther, how are you?"

"I'm fine, Ola. And you? You don't sound like yourself. What's wrong?"

"Well, I just got a letter from school today. They placed me on academic probation because of my grades," Ola answered.

Esther let out a long breath. "That's not good. What are you going to do?"

"I don't know, that's why I'm calling." Ola paced back and forth. "I have no idea what my next move should be."

"Don't you think you should change your major to something you like and understand better?" Esther said. "It's just, I never thought you would go into biology. You're so good at computers, and technology is a growing field. You could probably make even better money in tech than if you became a doctor. And you might not have to be in school that long." She paused, then started again more slowly. "Ola, listen to me: Being a doctor is a long-term commitment. It's a specialized field that takes a lot of hard work to succeed in. And it's not for everyone—people who become doctors have the innate desire to heal people. You can't slide by with a mild interest. You're either in or you're not."

"It might be a good idea to change it," Ola agreed. "I do love computers. I just never thought of it as a career." He heaved a sigh. "The problem is Mom and Dad. They want at least one of us to become a doctor."

"So?"

"Well, since I'm the youngest and you, Teresa, and Gabriel aren't going to become doctors, I thought it was my responsibility to fulfill that dream."

"Ola, at what cost would you fulfill a dream that isn't yours? We can't live for Mom and Dad. There are standards they would love us to meet, but our lives are our own. Listen, I've been where you are. Each of us has had the same conversation where we had to let Mom and Dad down about the doctor thing. After a while, they understand. And besides, all of us are successes in our way—and Gabriel's a lawyer. That's as close to a doctor as they're going to get from us."

"You know, maybe you're right," said Ola. "It's so stressful to keep going down this path that isn't my own."

"Remember, this is your life and no one else's," said Esther. "No one has to live with your decisions but you. And failure is part of the process. It teaches us lessons like you wouldn't believe, and it builds our character. Without failure, we would be stuck in a vicious cycle, not following our hearts."

Ola was silent for a long time, then said, "I'll think about it. Thanks, Esther."

"I'm not telling you what to do," she said, "but I think following your intuition is the best bet in this situation. Sit with it for a while, then make your decision. I know it'll be a good one."

"Okay."

Esther yawned. "Well, it's late, and I've got to be up early for work. Let's talk more tomorrow. Good night, Ola."

For hours afterward, Ola walked around campus contemplating his decision. A few days later, it was time to go back home for the summer.

After a couple of weeks, Ola decided to tell his parents he was changing his major. Esther was there when he broke the news and was able to help their parents accept Ola's decision. When fall semester arrived, Ola happily switched his major to computer science.

Not Following Your Intuition: Explanation
Morals vs. Ethics

What are the Mindless Behaviors?
We're influenced by the environment around us and the expectations the external world holds us to. Intuition is a feeling deep inside that leads to making decisions that either align with or go against our internal beliefs.

Some of our most intuitive and automatic reactions stem from believing our family knows best. Ola thought he needed to go to school for biology because it would make his parents proud. He strove for achievements he thought would make him successful based on the goals his family set forth. The fact that none of his other siblings were doctors just added to the pressure Ola felt. In the case of living up to family expectations, we often go against our intuition to please our external environments.

When we don't follow our intuition, we become complacent, pleasing the outside world without examining its values to ensure they align with our own. Even though Ola's close friends said it was a mistake for him to major in biology, he refused to go against his parents' wishes. For their part, Ola's parents wanted him to become a doctor not only to please themselves but to please their community through their son's impressive achievement. They believed being a doctor was one of the most lucrative career paths Ola could take without knowing his other options.

We can sometimes hang on to the expectations of another person's dream for a long time, even when it no longer serves us. Even though Ola was struggling with his courses and had difficulty grasping the concepts, he tried to continue with his major anyway. It was challenging for him to break free of his parents' expectations because their goals had become his own.

We spend so much time living to please the external world that we feel our own needs don't have value. Ola became voiceless by ignoring his passions and interests. He was repeatedly called on to fix computers and build systems for friends and relatives, but he refused to believe his hobby could have the same value—financial and social—as being a doctor. We never want to disappoint our family, especially our parents, so we often do things that can cause us a lot of pain in the name of making them happy. The external pressure can boil up so much that sometimes we have to go through extreme situations to break free.

Ola was unaware of how much going against his intuition was affecting his life, which led to him almost failing out of school. His story shows us how much our families can influence our decision-making, and how we can be blinded to our potential when we try to please the outside world.

Why do we cling to the Mindless Behaviors?
We're in a constant battle between what is ethically right versus morally right. Ethically, we make decisions based on what's right for our family and the environments we live in. Morally, decisions are made based on what serves our own talents and beliefs. At any given moment, we switch back and forth between ethics and morals based on the issues and environments in play.

Ola was stuck between fulfilling his parents' dreams versus living his own. It was clear the vision of Ola becoming a doctor was what his parents wanted and what he believed was ethically right for him. He didn't consider the moral standpoint and how it comes into play when making informed life decisions.

Being ethical means holding yourself accountable to the environment you serve, but it doesn't consider your moral side. Morals and ethics can sometimes conflict, as

Ola's did when he struggled with the idea of failing his parents. We inherit a lot of behavioral "garments" from the systems, traditions, cultures, and social norms we grow up with. Ola faced the difficult challenge of honoring his family wishes over his internal desire. There was an underlying fear that said, "If I don't go in this direction, my parents may be upset and disappointed in me."

Picture this: You're born into a family structure of some kind. You're taught the belief systems, values, traditions, ethics, history, and cultural norms of that family, many of which you don't question because of the perception that "this is how it is." Being a child comes with strict rules around how you should behave. Then adolescence hits—you're even more sensitive to the world, feeling a taste of social pressure, questioning your identity, and trying to understand where you fit in. More important, you're committing to dreams and goals that may not be your own. Finally, you assimilate to what your external world wants you to become, and you lose your intuition due to your limited sense of self.

Following our intuition is the least of our worries when we're exposed to environments that hand us our identities at birth and expect us to conform to them for life. I call this "the slave game," and the more entangled we get in it, the harder it is to find a way out. How can we create the life we want if a predetermined path was laid out for us before we were born?

The slave game is the debt we think we owe society, friends, family, and our communities when we don't follow our prescribed paths. It can manifest as shame, fear, or alienation. It leaves us powerless, surrendering to a system that doesn't work. In this game, we're made to believe we're winning even though there's always a system in place moving us around like chess pieces on a board.

How do we overcome mindlessness?
At times, our intuition challenges our inherited beliefs, which puts us in conflict with ourselves when it comes to making informed life decisions. Our internal alarm system goes off when our beliefs aren't aligned with our values.

Self-honesty is the key to gaining clarity about your life path. Ola wasn't honest with himself about his capacity to change his circumstances. He chose a major he didn't have an affinity for because of an external belief (his parents' dreams of having a doctor in the family). Furthermore, he wasn't honest with his parents about how much he was struggling at school. Ola didn't understand the severity of the situation until he was forced to face the deeper issue. When we're not honest with ourselves, we can't achieve our ultimate potential. Honesty

opens the doors to creative opportunities a
tial for an abundant life.

We're sometimes trained to overlook th
natural skill, an intense interest—becaus
supposed to focus on what we're told, espec
comes to career decisions. Unfortunately, we often abandon these passions to please the external worlds we live in. And when we put our passion on a shelf, we put part of our life with it.

But paying attention to your passions offers a deeper understanding of your direction. Our passions are very old and stem from things we loved to do during childhood. When we're passionate about something, it brings joy and energy to our souls.

Ola had been working on computers for as long as he could remember, but he didn't consider for a moment that he could do it for a living, even though he was getting paid to do it. The wants and needs of his environment overshadowed his passion.

Understanding the part family plays in your life can also give you great insights into your path. Family means different things to different people; whether it's a family we're born into or one we've acquired over time, our family is the foundation that shapes who we are. It's our support system, guiding us through good times and bad. Because of this, when it comes to making life decisions, e tend to fall back on what we learned in our families. However, some of the values our family possesses may not be our own, so it's up to us to form and follow our own value systems to make decisions. Esther helped Ola see the potential consequences of making decisions based on their parents' values. Their conversation shows how we all have the power to shape our lives if we trust our instincts and ourselves.

What can we learn from our Mindless Behaviors?
We stop clinging to this behavior when we start asking ourselves this tough question: Is living the way your environment tells you more important than following your values? Being honest with yourself in this way allows you to move in alignment with your intuition.

The message Esther gave Ola was an impactful one: you can't live your life for other people. At the end of the day, only you will have to live with the decisions you make. Take stock of what's going on in your life and it will show you how to move forward. Following your intuition begins by gaining a new understanding of the relationship you have with yourself.

Self-reflection questions to ask when you're not following your intuition:

- Is this the best decision for me?

_____

_____

_____

_____

- What do I really want to do?

_____

_____

_____

_____

_____

- What is my intuition trying to tell me about this situation?

_____

_____

_____

_____

Chapter Five

SEEKING A QUICK FIX

Coming to America had been Leica's dream since she was a little girl growing up in a small village in Venezuela. When the opportunity to live the American dream finally came in the form of marriage to her husband, Jimmy, she clung to it and promised to seize every moment.

Shortly after settling in Texas, Leica and Jimmy enrolled in night school. Leica dreamed of becoming a nurse, and Jimmy a teacher.

As they settled into married life, their responsibilities grew: paying bills, going to school, and eventually raising children. Leica and Jimmy were proud of their family and did everything to give them a better life than they'd had growing up.

After a few years, Jimmy dropped out of school to get a job to support the family while Leica went to school fulltime in order to finish. Money was tight, not only because they were living off one income but because Leica regularly sent money back home to support her family in Venezuela. Even after Leica graduated and found a well-paying nursing job, she and Jimmy fought constantly about finances. Leica felt that no matter how hard they worked, it still wasn't enough to keep the family afloat.

One evening, one of Leica's friends invited her to a casino for a girls' night out. That one night soon became occasional visits with her girlfriends, then solo trips. Eventually Leica was going to the casino by herself every week. She would win some and lose some; either way, she hid the visits from Jimmy. Deep down, she hoped that by gambling she could win enough money to pull the family out of their rut—enough to get ahead and truly relax for a change.

Keeping up with work and family and her gambling habit took a toll on Leica's health. She was in and out of the hospital for years with various ailments, but doctors couldn't pinpoint what was wrong. Her condition worsened over time to the point she could no longer keep up with her job. The more she went to the hospital, the less she worked, and the more financially unstable the family became.

Leica's hospital visits had another side effect: she began gambling even more to cope with her depression over her unexplained illnesses. Eventually she couldn't hide anymore. Her family discovered her gambling when a mortgage payment bounced. Jimmy sought help for Leica, which helped her addiction. But her overall health didn't seem to be getting better. Leica and Jimmy decided to take another approach and went to a research clinic a couple of hours from where they lived.

Sitting in the doctor's office, Leica waited patiently for her test results. After a few minutes, she began breathing heavily. She clutched her heart and whispered to Jimmy, "I can't breathe!"

"Hold on!" Jimmy said. "I'll get Dr. Reed!" He ran out of the room quickly and returned with a doctor and nurse in tow. When they opened the door, Leica was curled up on the floor, gasping for breath.

The doctor rushed to her side and laid her flat on the floor to check her vitals. "Don't worry, you're going to be okay, Mrs. Ramirez." He turned to the nurse. "We need to get her downstairs to Emergency."

Minutes later, orderlies wheeled a bed into the room and lifted Leica onto it. Jimmy stood in the corner helplessly, tears in his eyes. He watched his wife gasp for breath as the team of hospital workers abruptly left the room with Leica.

"Are you okay, Mr. Ramirez?" said the nurse.

"I'm just shaken up," Jimmy said.

"We'll take good care of her, Mr. Ramirez. Now come with me," said the nurse.

The nurse took Jimmy to the hospital's emergency wing. He waited patiently in the waiting room for nearly an hour with no news about Leica. Finally, Dr. Reed came back.

Jimmy jumped to his feet. "Dr. Reed, how is my wife doing?"

"We've stabilized her for the time being."

"What happened?" Jimmy said.

"She had a mild stroke."

"What? A stroke?"

"Luckily we caught it in time. We're a research clinic, and our primary goal is to get to the root of the problem. We're going to dive deep into the cause of her stroke, but to do that, we want to keep her under observation for at least the next couple of days."

"Is she going to be okay?" Jimmy asked, wringing his hands. "It's just that we've been through a lot with my wife's health. She has been in and out of the hospital, and it seems like she's not getting better."

Dr. Reed nodded sympathetically. "I understand. As I said, our process is to get to the root of what's wrong so we can treat her accordingly. We'll have some test results back tomorrow. Right now, she's sound asleep and in stable condition."

"Can you take me to her?" Jimmy asked.

"Of course," said Dr. Reed. "Come with me."

Dr. Reed led Jimmy down a series of hallways until

they reached Leica's room. When they entered, Leica was indeed sound asleep, just as Dr. Reed had said.

Dr. Reed stood behind Jimmy. "You really need to get some rest, Mr. Ramirez," he said. "We'll talk about the test results tomorrow." He left the room quietly, leaving Jimmy to watch Leica sleep for a few minutes in private. When he was sure she was breathing peacefully, he left and went back to the hotel he and Leica had been staying at to get some rest.

———

When Jimmy arrived at the hospital the following morning, Leica was up and alert. Jimmy was happy to see his wife doing well. After a couple of hours, Dr. Reed knocked on the door.

"Hello, Mr. and Mrs. Ramirez. How are you this morning?"

"Fine," they answered in unison.

"Mrs. Ramirez, after the incident in my office yesterday, we ran more tests to get a better understanding of your condition. We also researched all the medications you said you were taking. We realized something that came as a great shock: you've been misdiagnosed with a condition you don't have."

Leica's eyes widened as Jimmy clutched her hand.

"Dr. Reed, what are you saying?" Leica asked. "Misdiagnosed how?"

"You have chronic obstructive pulmonary disease, or COPD, not asthma," said Dr. Reed. "We can treat it with medication, but we'll have to go slowly. Right now, you're on a lot of different types of meds. Before we can start adding new ones, we need to ease you off the ones you're on gradually."

"Why do you have to take me off the meds slowly if I don't need them?" Leica asked.

"The medication's affecting your system and individual organ function. If we take you off them cold turkey, your body could go into shock."

Leica and Jimmy sat in stunned silence. After a long moment, Leica found her voice. "So, what happens to me now?"

Dr. Reed's face was grave. "I'm afraid there's nothing we can do for you now but start the process of weaning you off the asthma meds. You'll also need to come in at least twice a month for checkups until we get this sorted out."

Leica started crying, and Jimmy put his arm around her. "Doctor, was this something that could've been caught earlier on?" he asked.

The doctor nodded. "Yes, Mr. Ramirez, your wife's previous doctors should've caught this." He turned to face Leica. "You were in and out of the hospital because no one tried to address the root of your problems, they simply treated the symptoms with more and more medication. Now your body is paying the price. If you weren't here in the hospital when you had that mini stroke, the outcome could've been much worse."

"How long will I be in the hospital?" Leica asked.

"I can't give you an exact timeline right now, unfortunately. We'll need to conduct a few more tests to determine the extent of your COPD. And remember, you're still recovering from a stroke. My best guess is that you'll be with us for at least a few more days." Dr. Reed stood to leave. When he reached the doorway, he stopped and turned around. "I'm sorry, Mrs. Ramirez. Truly I am." And with that, he left the couple to deal with the fallout from his news.

_____

The next day, Jimmy and Leica sat in her hospital room, still shocked by the news.

"What are we going to do now? We can't afford to be coming to Mercy twice a month for checkups," Leica said.

"It's your health, Leica," said Jimmy. "We've got to find a way."

"I can't afford to miss work like this," Leica griped. As she stared out the window, tears welled in her eyes. "How could I have missed the signs? I'm a nurse! It's my job to take care of people and make sure patients get the best treatment. We were trained to trust doctors. I've seen this happen to patients, but I never thought it would happen to me."

Jimmy smiled sadly. "No one ever does."

Leica stared down at her hands twisting together in her lap. "Jimmy, I see now that I was deep in denial. I wasn't willing to face the challenges in front of me, so I looked for anything to distract myself, not understanding the long-term consequences. But this situation has really made me think about how I see things. I need to take care of myself more. It seems like I abandoned my needs and placed my faith in a flawed system."

"You can point blame at anyone, but in the end, you're left holding all the pieces," Jimmy said. "Yes, it sucks that you were misdiagnosed, but now we can find a way to heal and grow, together. I'm hopeful."

Leica smiled through her tears. "I love you so much. I'm sorry for everything I did. It wasn't fair to you and the kids."

"We're family, Leica!" Jimmy answered. "We'll find a way."

Seeking Quick Fixes: Explanation
Band-Aids vs. Roots

What are the Mindless Behaviors?
When we're stuck in a rut, we tend to find short-term solutions to deep-rooted problems. Our judgment is impaired, which puts us in a constant state of treating a problem rather than solving it. Short-term solutions come from improper research, impatience, and carelessness in losing sight of the roots of the issue at hand. We lose sight of how to make constructive decisions when we're stuck in a rut or in pain. As a result, we're blindsided by people who may be affected by the decision we make. Leica failed to communicate her feelings and the pain she was going through with her family, which caused a breakdown in her health and family dynamics. Leica and Jimmy constantly fought about finances, which created a communication barrier within their relationship. She went into isolation, letting no one, not even her husband, see the pain she felt due to the conflicts in the household.

Leica didn't understand the full effect her short-term decisions to gamble would have on the environment she lived in. Her gambling addiction stemmed from not having enough and always worrying about providing for her family and relatives back in her hometown. Financial problems became habitual and quickly grew worse, but Leica didn't really understand the consequences of her gambling addiction until it started to bankrupt her family. She adopted a mindset of "If I win, my family will finally be free from financial worries." This thought alone—the possibility of gaining financial freedom—spurred Leica to gamble countless times.

As Leica used gambling as a mental getaway from her deep-rooted issues, her physical health deteriorated, pushing her further down the rabbit hole. She was in and out of the hospital for years only to find out she was misdiagnosed. Her doctors kept treating her conditions instead of finding permanent solutions. And the more Leica's health faded, the more she gambled. It was all intertwined with the unfortunate events that transpired in the story.

Our toxic environments can put people in a state of always seeking instant gratification. When things become challenging and unbearable, we're especially prone to looking for short-term solutions to make the problem go away. Our world is very reactive; we're continually stimulated by everything around us, which prohibits us from digging deeper into our thoughts to come up with sustainable solutions to our problems.

Why do we cling to the Mindless Behaviors?

In the state of finding solutions to problems, our judgments are at times impaired, setting us on a collision course between Band-Aids and Roots. Band-Aids are solutions made with short-term results in mind. They're thinking of a problem in the moment and making impulsive decisions without gathering insights about potential long-term effects. Roots, on the other hand, address problems from multiple angles and are based on a deep understanding of the situation at hand.

These days, there are more Band-Aids out there than Roots. The issue stems from living in environments that unconsciously look at problems from one perspective. Looking at a problem through one lens too often keeps people stuck with the same problems.

Leica didn't fully understand the long-term effects of her addiction. She didn't realize that the more money she gambled away, the less she would have. Clinging to the possibility of financial freedom increased her urge to gamble, which led to a host of financial problems. Leica's constant financial struggles, the pressure of supporting relatives and caring for a family, and her deteriorating health caused her to have a lack of vision, low self-worth, and constant fear about what tomorrow might bring. When in pain, we find things to take the hurt away at any cost, even if our health suffers in the end.

As a result of all the stresses in her life and the constant worry about supporting her family, Leica abandoned her health, causing another set of problems to arise. Leica was in and out of the hospital, but each time the doctors provided her with medications that temporarily relieved her condition without solving the root causes. This shows that seeking quick fixes isn't just a mindless behavior for individuals; it's a systematic issue we face every day. Our systems are set up to seek surface solutions before tackling the roots.

Leica was in a constant state of fear, living from one moment to another and clinging to the hope of resolving her condition. The doctors' mismanagement of her health led her to question everything around her. As she stated at the end of the story, "I've seen this happen to other people, but I never thought it would happen to me." This statement shows how far we can go astray even when we have the tools to change our circumstances. Leica trusted the doctors to provide her with excellent care even though she had the medical background to diagnose herself. Overall, it seems as if she gave up and gave in to the problems she faced in her life.

Complacency can cause us to cling to mindless behaviors, and not knowing how to pull ourselves out increases the problem drastically. Since a scarcity mindset consistently resurfaced throughout the story, it's clear there was some complacency around the struggles Leica and her family experienced. In other words, Leica was in denial, which trapped her in a complex web of financial, physical, and emotional problems.

How do we overcome mindlessness?
It's important to look at a problem through multiple lenses before making an informed decision. We're sometimes too quick to pass judgment on issues we haven't thoroughly researched, or to react to situations when we're in a state of turmoil.

When Leica married and moved to the United States, she assumed a massive load of new responsibilities as a nurse, wife, mother, and student. She reacted by viewing the situation from only one perspective: "To be a good person, I must take on these duties without fail." The more she ignored the root problem—burnout and overwork, in her case—and sought short-term solutions to fix it, the greater the problem became. Taking a narrow viewpoint when making decisions can bring us down paths that are worse than the ones we're already on.

Understanding the pain of your problems can lead to getting out of them faster. Constant pain impairs our decision-making skills, so it's important to understand the emotional baggage that comes with your pain, especially when the pain is reoccurring in different ways.

Leica didn't fully understand her pain and the condition she was putting her family in by gambling her money away. She was using the quick fix of gambling to ease her problems, avoiding the far deeper pain she was feeling. Financial instability, conflict with her husband, an inability to communicate clearly, and a host of mysterious medical conditions were too much for Leica to handle—ignoring the pain was easier than facing it head-on.

Finding solutions by seeking guidance from your support networks can offer a way out of tough situations. Whether it's professional help or friendly advice, seeking outside help can give you more perspective about your problems. One of the major roots of Leica's problems was money, which can be a challenging subject to talk about in our society. People often hesitate to discuss their finances openly, particularly if they're experiencing financial problems. Societal taboos like this can lead people like Leica to mask their problems with short-term solutions instead of looking for a cure.

Trading the scarcity mindset for an abundance mindset can also lead to better decision-making. This is the most challenging step to take because of our society's constant message of "not enough"—not enough time, money, possessions, friends, and so on. Leica came to the United States to build a "better" life; her sense of never having enough, being enough, or feeling enough kept her clinging to the behaviors. Many people experience these "not enough" feelings in different ways every day without realizing it, which can lead them to try to fill themselves up in the form of addictions like shopping, substance abuse, emotional drama, and much more.

What can we learn from our Mindless Behaviors?
We can't control the environments we're subjected to every day. Different problems will always arise, but it's up to us to find a way to gain clarity about the conditions we live in. When we ignore our problems, they can spiral out of control, as Leica's story illustrated.

At times, a problem may come that's too overwhelming for you to handle. That's when it's important to reach out to individuals you trust and/or professionals for deeper insight into what to do. When we feel supported and unafraid to speak our truth, we can move mountains. But even though you have a community to rely on, remember, you're the one who has the final word on how your life will turn out. So play the doctor by finding your own cures for your problems.

Self-reflection questions to ask when you encounter quick fixes:

- What's the real root of this problem?

_____

_____

_____

_____

- How can I find my own "cure" for this situation?

_____

_____

_____

_____

- Is this solution a Band-Aid or a Root?

_____

_____

_____

_____

_____

Chapter Six

LETTING PAST EXPERIENCES AFFECT THE PRESENT

Bryan's heart shattered the day he learned Lydia, his girlfriend of four years, had died the night before. Red roses turned black when a future that was once so bright took an unfortunate turn.

Her death sent shockwaves through their community. Overwhelmed by grief, Bryan decided not to attend the funeral. The memories of their relationship played in his mind like a never-ending symphony.

One year later, Bryan decided to move out of state to make a fresh start. Everywhere he turned reminded him of Lydia, and he wanted to put the past behind him. His friends and family were initially against the move; they thought he was still mourning Lydia and wasn't stable enough to leave. But they accepted the decision eventually.

Bryan found a new job, packed his bags, and moved to Cincinnati. Over the next year and a half, life and work were good to him. He began to feel more like his old self, so much so that when he saw a beautiful woman sitting alone at his neighborhood bar, he got up the nerve to approach her. It turned out they were neighbors—Rebecca lived just one building complex over from Bryan. They hit it off that night and started to talk regularly.

They'd been dating for several months when Rebecca broached the subject of their relationship over dinner at their favorite restaurant. "So," she said, "what's the next step for you and me?"

Bryan choked on his wine. "Next step? Honey, I thought we both agreed to keep things casual."

"Well sure, at the beginning," Rebecca said. "But my feelings have changed since then. Haven't yours? I mean, we text all the time, we see each other almost every day. Are you saying the thought of moving in together never crossed your mind?"

Bryan didn't say anything. In truth, he had thought about asking Rebecca to move in with him. But the possibility of getting close to another woman scared him.

Rebecca interrupted his thoughts. "Bryan, I can't do this anymore if there's no progress. Neither of us are getting any younger, and it'll just get too complicated if we stay in this casual dating zone." She paused, then met his eyes. "I think we need a break. A long break."

———

Rebecca was true to her word: weeks passed with no

communication from her. After a long, lonely month, Bryan finally decided to call her.

He expected her to let the call go to voicemail, but she picked up on the second ring. "Hello."

"Hey, it's me."

"I know. Why are you calling?"

Bryan took a deep breath. "I want to clear the air. Can I come over?"

There was a long silence. Then, "Sure. I'm not promising anything, but I'm open to hearing what you have to say."

"Understood."

Bryan practically sprinted to Rebecca's apartment. When he got there, they sat on the couch to talk.

"Look, I know neither of us was looking for a long-term relationship when we met," said Rebecca. "But after a while, I began to catch feelings. My heart's changed—now I know I really do want a partner I can be with forever." She turned away from him to stare at the floor. "I thought if we took a break I could get comfortable with the idea of just being friends. Maybe that'll happen someday, but not now. It just hurts too much."

Bryan reached for her hand. "Rebecca, a lot has happened to me in the past few years that I'm still sorting through, the main thing being . . ." He took a deep breath, then forged ahead. "Before I moved here, I was seeing a girl named Lydia. We were together for four years. She died unexpectedly."

Rebecca stared at him. "That's awful. I'm so sorry. Why didn't you ever tell me?"

Bryan kept talking as if he hadn't heard her. "My world fell apart when I found out. What really hurt was that she called me right before she died. We had a fight a few days before that—she thought I wasn't interested in taking the relationship to the next level. I was actually planning to propose to her that summer—I just needed more time to save up for the ring. But because of that stupid fight . . ." Bryan hung his head. "I was just so mad."

"All relationships have ups and downs," Rebecca said. "You couldn't have known she would get into an accident when you had the fight."

"It's not just that," Bryan said. "Lydia called me the night of her death. I saw her name on my phone, but I ignored it. I was still mad over the fight, plus I was out drinking with some friends. After a couple of hours, though, I decided to see what she wanted. I listened to the message—she said it was an emergency and insisted I call her back, which I did, but it kept going to voicemail. Then her sister called and said Lydia had died." Tears started falling down Bryan's face. "It turned out she was having an ectopic pregnancy. When she called me, she was looking for a ride to the hospital because she was in so much pain."

"Oh my god, Bryan, I'm so sorry. That must've been so hard for you. There are no words. No words," said Rebecca, tearing up.

"I didn't even know she was pregnant," Bryan murmured. "When I found out, I was devastated. It was like someone ripped my heart out. For a while I could barely function. I didn't even go to the funeral. It was just too much to bear, knowing I could've saved her if I wasn't too stubborn to pick up my phone that night."

"Listen to me, Bryan: it wasn't your fault," Rebecca said. "Yes, you guys fought, but it's natural for people in relationships to have conflicts now and then. Your pain is real, and you have to give yourself permission to feel it. Telling me your story is a huge start. You managed to find words to talk about the unspeakable. To me, that means you're finally ready to heal, and heal in a way you never knew you could."

Bryan sighed. "When I moved here, I swore I'd never be in a relationship or get close to anyone again."

"Bryan, you can't just push everyone away because of what happened with Lydia. If you don't face your pain, nobody will stand a chance of starting a relationship with you." She squeezed his hand. "And there are some of us who'd really like that chance."

Bryan gave a small smile. "You know, maybe you're right," he said. "But where do I start after all these years of bottling everything up?"

"Well, have you been back home since you moved?"

"No, not for years," Bryan said.

"Then maybe you should visit and try to come to terms with things. Only if you're ready, of course," Rebecca said. "Either way, thank you for telling me. I really appreciate your openness." She hugged Bryan and kissed him on the cheek, whispering, "Whatever happens, I'll be here for you."

———

Soon after, Bryan decided to go home for a visit. Rebecca was thrilled with his decision. Bryan's family and friends were shocked to see him, but they welcomed him with open arms. After a couple of days of catching up, he visited Lydia's grave to pay his respects. Leaving the graveyard, he felt a sense of deep peace, like a weight had been lifted from his heart. When Bryan went back to Cincinnati, he told Rebecca all about the experience over dinner in their new shared apartment.

Letting Past Experiences Affect the Present: Explanation

Our Lessons vs. Our Bitterness

What are the Mindless Behaviors?

When we're in deep pain, we unconsciously carry our emotional baggage from the past without thinking through how it affects our new circumstances. Our actions can negatively impact others when we haven't come to terms with our pain. In this story, Bryan pushed away everything and everyone that reminded him of Lydia and the life they shared, worrying his friends and family and coloring his perception of his relationship with Rebecca.

Clear communication is shattered when we're in a turbulent state. Our minds are so paralyzed by trauma that interacting with our environments in a healthy way is the furthest thing from our minds. Bryan's guilt over Lydia's death drove him to isolate himself from others for a long time. Like Bryan, we all use different tools—distraction, denial, and so forth—to escape the shock and regret we feel in moments of vulnerability. Unable to deal with our pain directly, we jump into relationships prematurely, abuse substances, and commit other self-destructive acts. When we're too angry to even acknowledge our pain, the effect on our environments can be even more detrimental, as when Bryan's past colored his relationship with Rebecca. It's hard to deal with old hurts, especially if you feel you're at fault.

Conditional intimate relationships, inherited family behaviors, betrayals, shattered dreams, broken hearts, and manufactured social conflicts all contribute to this behavior. During tough times, communication usually breaks down, which creates mental barriers that trap people and prohibit them from fully articulating their pain.

Why do we cling to the Mindless Behaviors?
Most of the time, we humans oscillate between learning lessons from painful experiences or growing bitter over them. Our lessons come from observing past hurts from different perspectives and applying any nuggets of wisdom we gain to the next situation. Bitterness, on the other hand, stems from not fully processing a bad situation, which opens up the possibility of staying stuck in trauma even when the moment has passed.

Bryan's guilt was unconsciously making him bitter. He had trouble opening up and communicating his feelings, as well as a major fear of commitment. By trying to suppress his pain over Lydia's death, he resisted any chance of learning from the past.

We do anything to protect ourselves from the pain of traumatic experiences, even pushing away those closest to us. But avoiding unresolved grief in one relationship or situation only makes room for it to manifest unconsciously later on. Our bitterness stems from not understanding a situation for what it is. It's living in denial that's at times self-inflicted but also hurts the environments we live in.

Bryan and Rebecca's story was about an intimate relationship, but there are many kinds of relationships that fall prey to bitterness: parent/child relationships, friendships, business partnerships, sibling relationships, relationships with coworkers, and finally your relationship with yourself. At some point we're all guilty of clinging to mindless behaviors and letting the past negatively affect the present.

How do we overcome mindlessness?
Relationships teach us the power of understanding people and their unique journeys through life. Every relationship we encounter is valuable on multiple levels.

When we experience deep trauma, it's easy to blame others without examining the part we played in the situation or considering which actions were within our control. Bryan realized the loss of Rebecca hurt more than coming clean about what was bothering him. Their conversation helped him sit with the pain and understand it from a different perspective.

Trauma can be unconsciously inflicted when bringing past bad experiences into new relationships. We have a natural negative reaction when we put our hearts into something and it doesn't come out the way we hoped. But holding on to anger from a previous relationship keeps us from looking at our new situation from a different perspective.

Sitting with our anger gives us permission to unpack our fear and dive deeper into what's really bothering us. Anger is a powerful emotion; it alters the way we handle situations by keeping our focus on the negatives. It allows us to lash out in ways that leave a thick trail of bitterness at the end of the experience.

Bryan was angry because he wasn't there for Lydia in her time of need, and he blamed himself for her death. His anger and guilt undermined his relationship with Rebecca, making him reluctant to share his feelings. At times, we can be angry and not even know it until a situation sparks a negative emotion. Bryan's story teaches us to face our fears and to make sense of our anger in order for the lessons to come through.

Clear communication is vital to fostering healthy relationships and moving them to a deeper level. But communication can be a challenge due to the invisible restrictions around emotions.

Historically, as human beings, we've enacted many unspoken rules that prohibit us from expressing emotions like pain in a constructive way. This can be especially true for men, who often have to deal with stereotypes that deride emotion as unmasculine. Bryan suppressed the pain of losing Lydia by moving to a different state, not clearly communicating with his support network, and even hiding his feelings from Rebecca.

When we experience pain, we often feel ashamed and convince ourselves we're alone. Patterns can be broken when we scrutinize our behavior to understand the part we play in healing from the trauma.

What can we learn from our Mindless Behaviors?
By understanding problems are finite and that we have the power to overcome tough situations, our lives can improve in a way that brings us peace. With relationships, we must understand we're worthy of having them in our lives. Worth starts with understanding our place in the world and believing we have unique and valuable contributions to make to society. Our painful experience of the past doesn't last forever, and each experience teaches us a lesson that can accelerate our growth.

Forgiveness is part of growth, and it's something we need to embrace even in our darkest moments. It's brave to forgive trauma, but an even braver act is to understand the lessons behind our experiences, so we don't repeat them.

Self-reflection questions to ask when you allow past experiences to affect the present:

- Are there past experiences I haven't gotten over?

- Is it worth it to carry the pain of a situation when it no longer serves me?

- How can I move forward in breaking this cycle?

_____

_____

_____

_____

_____

_____

Chapter Seven

LIVING IN PANDEMONIUM

Marjorie sat in the corner of a pitch-black room, tied up in a straitjacket. A thin beam of light came from a tiny window in the door, her only access to the outside world.

Marjorie yelled at the top of her lungs, "Get me out of here!"

Nothing.

She got up to peer through the glass circle. Out in the hallway, her father was talking to one of the doctors. She banged on the door and yelled again, "Get me out of here!"

The doctor and her father looked up, then turned back to their conversation.

Marjorie paced back and forth until she was out of breath. Exhausted, she lay down in the middle of the room and slowly dosed off.

After a couple of hours, the doctors came in to take her to another room to get some rest. Marjorie was so tired she didn't have the strength to fight them. She hadn't slept in three days, fighting to stay up to see what was going on.

The next morning, Marjorie was wide awake. The doctors came in to check on her due to her behavior the night before. She was fully alert and ready to go home, but the doctors, worried about her mental state, placed a forty-eight-hour hold on her and insisted she get more rest. They also told her they'd need to run multiple tests before she could leave the psych ward.

With nowhere to go for the next forty-eight hours, Marjorie started reflecting on her life. She wanted to make sure she never saw this place ever again. Ideas slowly started to manifest in her mind now that she had rested. When her test results came back, the doctors realized Marjorie was suffering from extreme sleep deprivation. They also diagnosed her with bipolar disorder; she didn't agree with them, but she didn't make a fuss because she was itching to get out of the ward.

Seventy-two hours passed before Marjorie was finally released. She was thrilled to finally be out of the psych ward. Her dad picked her up and took her to her apartment. She finally got her phone back and quickly checked her missed messages from the past few days. One was from her boss, insisting she call him immediately.

Once she'd gotten settled and her dad had finally left, Marjorie called her boss. After she explained what had happened, he decided to release her from her position due to the "terrible scene" Marjorie made shortly before going to the psych ward. She was actually relieved—the position had been a source of intense stress in her life. But the reality that her primary income was no more hadn't sunk in yet.

The moment she got off the phone with her boss, she called her friend Elizabeth, who insisted on coming over to talk. Within an hour, she was at Marjorie's door.

"Hey, thanks for coming," Marjorie said.

"Always!" Elizabeth said. "Hey, what's that amazing smell?"

"Lemon pepper chicken, rice, and veggies. It's almost done. Do you want some?"

"Sure, I would love some. What made you want to cook?"

"I needed to do something to clear my mind, and it's too cold out for a walk."

"Well it smells great." Elizabeth put her purse down on the kitchen counter and looked at Marjorie with concern. "So, how are you doing? I was worried about you," she said.

"I'm okay. I'm just taking things day by day."

"What happened? You were acting a little off before . . ."

"It's okay, you can say it: before I went to the psych

ward," Marjorie said. "I was tired, overwhelmed, and stressed from work, and then this ex of mine trying to come back just put me over the edge."

"That's not good. I told you to stay away from that boy!" said Elizabeth.

"He's not the problem. It's everything else. I'm tired. Do you know how stressful it is to be a woman in her thirties whose only stable relationship is with a job that's grinding her into dust? I might always have a smile on my face—I try to embrace every obstacle as a lesson—but I've gotten to the point of saying to myself, How did I get here? Is this really my life?"

"Wow, sounds like you've got a lot on your mind," Elizabeth said.

"Yeah, working ninety-hour weeks and flying to different states every month to represent a heartless company will do that to you. Do you know they told me today they're releasing me from my contract?"

"What? That's crazy! You've given so much of your time to them," Elizabeth said.

"Yes, four years of it. Crazy, huh? In every job I've ever had, I've had to continually prove I had the right to be there. It's time for me to create my own opportunities, ones that allow me to dance in my creativity and show my value. The only way I can do that is to go out into the world and try to find my place." She sighed heavily.

"Everybody thinks I have it together, but I really don't. It's like no one understands me well enough to see how much I'm struggling."

"I'm sorry you're feeling this way," Elizabeth said. "You know you can always talk to me, right?"

"I know. At the lowest point in my breakdown, I had a breakthrough. I suddenly became aware of my surroundings. I started to have dreams of which direction I could take my life in, and ideas I want to bring to life. I'm beginning to understand that everything I'm going through is due to a lack of awareness. People these days just aren't aware of their condition."

"Yeah, I know," agreed Elizabeth. "We're all so used to acting without thinking. But I don't think you should feel responsible for holding all this inside. Channeling your thoughts into something positive might help ease the pressure you're feeling. You could try meditation, yoga, a new hobby. The sky's the limit."

Marjorie nodded. "I think the first thing I'm going to do is build my brand. I want to talk to other people about building self-awareness. Unconscious bias is a massive problem with humanity; without the proper skills to make informed decisions, we're bound to keep repeating the same mistakes."

"Where would you start?" Elizabeth asked.

"Well, I've started putting together a business plan. I

know building a new brand takes time, but I'm up for the challenge," Marjorie said.

"Sounds like a great idea—I'm excited for you!" Elizabeth smiled brightly; then her face grew serious. "Listen, I'm sorry about everything that happened this week. For what it's worth, I believe all of us are fighting a lot of battles other people aren't aware of. It's up to each of us to be open to speaking the truth of what's going on inside."

Marjorie nodded. "I get what you're saying. But what if you've been talking and nobody's listening? What do you say then?"

———

A couple of years passed, and Marjorie finally launched her platform. She started holding master classes on self-awareness, and she found different ways to articulate her messages. It was a long time in the making, but her dream had finally come true.

At the final event of her first year in business, the room was filled with old faces and new. In this session, which had over sixty people in attendance, she was walking people through the behavior of living in pandemonium.

Marjorie used her ability to work the room to keep everyone engaged in the message. The crowd was eager to learn something new before exiting the event. She instructed the students to write a letter to themselves about their chaos, then read hers aloud as an example:

Dear Marjorie,

The life you live is rich—full of chaos, pain, adventures, ups, downs, and most of all, memorable moments. You're the daughter of brilliant immigrants who came to America over thirty-five years ago. Far from their homeland, your parents' greatest hope was to build a better life for themselves and their children. In many ways, they achieved this. Unfortunately, they left chaos behind only to meet it in different forms in their new country. This was chaos you couldn't comprehend unless you grew up and experienced it for yourself. And boy, you grew up fast!

As you got older, you learned your skin tone was a mark against you, your intelligence rendered you invisible, and your gender automatically made you a second-class citizen. All these challenges confined you to a mental cage of never-ending chaos: dead-end jobs, toxic relationships, emotional barriers, fear-based choices, complacency—you were a proud servant to a system that didn't serve you.

How did you navigate this world? By teaching yourself how to stand on the shoreline without ever dipping a toe in the ocean. You went only where you were tolerated and excelled at being less than your perfect. You lived on autopilot, hiding your anger until one tremendously stressful day when everything changed. You felt beyond angry, so much so that you shattered your favorite watch into a thousand pieces.

In that moment, your paradigm shattered. It was like the blinders you once had on were lifted. Time became abundant, not scarce. You broke down your emotional barriers. You danced in your creativity. You claimed your power and took nothing less than what you deserved. You faced your fears and finally started showing up for your life!

You could've easily chosen a path leading to self-destruction, but instead you decided to walk the path of compassion. It's so hard to maintain peace and balance in a world full of malice. You have the gift to impact your inner and outer world, which makes you a potent being. My message to you is to keep going on your journey. As you do, be thankful for everyone around you—they're all mirrors pushing you to become the best version of yourself. And remember, no matter what you're going through in life, you have the tools to overcome. You're the one you've been waiting for.

With love, Marjorie

Living in Pandemonium: Explanation
Blame vs. Accountability

What are the Mindless Behaviors?
Our chaotic lives stem from the idea that we should conform to social norms. This ideology leaves us complacent in many ways, chasing others' expectations and ideals instead of our own. Marjorie was living in pandemonium when she came to a breaking point in her career and personal life. As a result, she began to question her self-worth, which led to changing her direction in life. In the conversation with her friend, Marjorie mentioned that she ignored the signs she was struggling and kept

pressing ahead as if the situation would fix itself. She ignored her own needs to nurture things that didn't serve her well-being or higher purpose.

Marjorie felt lost in her own life. She eventually realized she had to take her power back and remove the mask she was wearing to please the people around her. A lot of us are like Marjorie, constantly running on empty to keep up with the high expectations of our environment until we eventually break down from sickness, burnout, problematic relationships, health issues, and the list goes on. Our identity is wrapped up in what the external world wants us to be.

When chaos arises in our lives, we tend to box ourselves into a mental cage, believing there's no escaping the situation. The problem gets bigger, but it's never cleaned up; chaos becomes a way of life, along with the inability to fix problems as they arise.

There's the old idea that time can heal any situation we're going through. Too many times, however, we doom a situation before we even take part in it. When we tell ourselves, "I can't do this," "This is too challenging," or "I give up!" we give the situation we're trying to solve power over our life.

Marjorie gave up control of her life by putting herself in situations she felt trapped within. The energy she put into her work and personal life wasn't an even exchange in the end, leaving her exhausted and confused. She was stuck and needed a breakthrough, which was illustrated in the story.

Chaos thrives when we feel there's no outlet to express our opinion, when we lack enough support to get out of tough situations, and when we fear judgment. Living in pandemonium is a form of living in constant chaos, with everything around you off-kilter or not to your satisfaction. At the core of this behavior is the inability to face problems head-on and a desire to shift the blame for our problems onto others.

Why do we cling to the Mindless Behaviors?
In chaos, we constantly waver between blaming others versus taking responsibility for our actions. It's the thinness of the line between the two concepts that keeps us in regular conflict with ourselves.

Blaming others or situations for our problems is a way of protecting our negative emotions. It keeps mirrors smoky when we cling to the idea that someone or something is to blame for our circumstances. Accountability is the idea of taking responsibility for the part we play in different situations, even if we're not at fault. There's a sense of understanding there's a lesson to be learned from the situations and the motivation to come up with solutions to clean up the mess.

We play the blame game with our upbringing, past hurts, and social circle to alleviate the pressure of not facing our present circumstances. Our decisions become reactive (that is, measured against the goals and expectations of others), and we put ourselves on autopilot, unaware of the chaos simmering just below the surface. The more we refuse to come to terms with our situation, the worse it becomes. When one problem is cured, another one arises to take its place.

We often believe, consciously or subconsciously, that we don't have control over our lives and that everyone else is to blame for our lack of progress or direction. In truth, there are powerful social systems in place that push us to project our responsibilities onto others. Marjorie inherited an outlook from her family, social groups, and business colleagues that kept her pointing fingers to explain why her life wasn't better.

Another reason we cling to this behavior is society's tendency to dehumanize people through a "survival of the fittest" mentality. Take Marjorie's firing, for example: even though she explained why she'd been absent from work and was a good worker, in the end her employer fired her. While there were likely many reasons behind Marjorie's abrupt dismissal, when we look deeper, we see that the core issue is that a human being was treated as a disposable object and not a precious jewel. This mindset arises through our society's push for constant competition, whether it's between countries, businesses, or individuals. Even though Marjorie was barely affected by losing her job, it raises a lot of questions about the world we live in.

Being "normal" is a constant battle because it constantly puts the "obvious path" laid out in front of us in conflict with our authentic self. In the story, Marjorie pointed out the mindlessness of her reactive decision-making. As she explained, she clung to assumptions without considering the long-term effect of staying on the obvious path.

A lot of us regularly feel emotional chaos like Marjorie, which can make us believe there's no hope of moving past obstacles or achieving our goals. We infect our minds with negative self-talk, distorted visons, and false perceptions that keep us stuck in a mental landfill.

How do we overcome mindlessness?
Overcoming this mindless behavior starts with taking accountability for the part we play in creating chaos in our lives. It's all too easy to point fingers instead of taking responsibility, especially when many of our social structures discourage us from doing so; this is likely due to the level of courage it takes to say, "Part of this is my fault."

Marjorie realized she had the ability to change her

life. The mirror she turned on herself became clearer as she stepped into her power and picked up her life one piece at a time. Becoming more reflective about our decision-making can limit the chaos in our lives.

Our world is full of individuals complying with rules they don't agree with—how to dress, whom to befriend, which job to take, and so on. Over time we become comfortable with these rules without understanding how they might be affecting our lives.

Marjorie was making decisions based on what she thought was socially correct. Even with red flags in front of her, the fear of going in a different direction was so foreign that sitting in her troubles was easier than facing them. This autopilot mode can land people in a web of circumstances that are beyond their control. It's important to think through your options carefully. When we sit with information we're trying to process, we bring greater clarity to the situations we're trying to solve.

It's important to find the lesson within the pandemonium so you can avoid it in the future. Unfortunately, lessons are the hardest things to see when you're trapped in the belly of chaos.

Marjorie saw many patterns in her life that led to her breakdown. Through self-reflection and the lessons she learned along the way, she was able to map a clear path to where she wanted to take her life on her own terms.

The lessons pointed out her shortcomings and opened her up to other opportunities she had within her to make a fruitful life. Learning lessons can be messy, but it's necessary for growth.

There's a sense of checking out that happens when you live in chaos. We give up on things that really matter to us because we feel rudderless. We conceal the turmoil from people close to us because we fear being exposed or misunderstood, as Marjorie did when she hid her problems from friends and family. But showing up for life and communicating with your inner circle can help you clean up the chaos faster.

It's easy to say no one is supportive, but at times, we don't give our support group the opportunity to understand us in a way that might allow them to provide helpful advice. We put false images of ourselves out there for the world to see, thinking that if we reveal our true self, no one will love us. Our self-judgment and refusal to give others a chance to help us keeps us trapped in a landfill of replicable problems. In the end, we haunt our own lives by only doing just enough to get by. Our fears are in our heads, and the excuses we make are hollow. Communication is a two-way street; we only receive messages we send out.

What can we learn from our Mindless Behaviors?
Marjorie's story shows how far astray we can go when our direction isn't clear and we ignore our problems. We stop clinging to the behavior of living in constant chaos when we realize it no longer serves us.

Recognizing the signs of chaos early and making informed decisions will put you on the path to decluttering your emotional baggage. Because when we allow unresolved emotional baggage to accumulate and continually run on autopilot, we rob ourselves of the human experience.

Also remember that our thoughts have a way of shaping our reality. Understanding the power of thinking—negative and positive—and exploring the issues you'd rather ignore is another way to clear out the chaos in your life.

Self-reflection questions to ask when you're living in pandemonium:

- What part did I play in creating this pandemonium?

_____

_____

_____

_____

- What is "normal" to me? Where did my idea of "normal" come from?

_____

_____

_____

_____

_____

- What can I do to bring more calm to this chaotic situation?

_____

_____

_____

_____

_____

_____

THE GOD WITHIN
Light vs. Darkness

Over the five years I wrote this book, I had to come to terms with my own mindless behaviors. Through my journey, I realized how much I was affected by my environment and the unchecked trauma I've experienced over the years.

Some of this trauma was self-inflicted, but some wasn't. In the midst of my journey, after three weeks in detention, my father got deported back to his home country of Nigeria with only the clothes on his back and thirteen dollars in his wallet. I was heartbroken. Immigration put him on a plane in the middle of the night; my family didn't know his whereabouts until he called us from the airport to tell each one of his children goodbye.

My father's story began over twenty years ago with an act of kindness: offering a friend in need an opportunity to make some money. This little seed grew into a sprawling tree of betrayal, sadness, financial challenges, overwhelming legal issues, and eventually his deportation.

Every type of emotion came over me the night I found out my father was being sent away: anger, fear, pain, confusion. All I could do was sit in bed crying. A man who'd been in this country for almost forty years, who'd raised a family, worked hard, and been a loyal friend to many had been forced out without a second thought. Afterward, I wondered over and over, How did we get here? Then, it dawned on me: we got here because we were unaware.

By sitting in my pain, I gained a different perspective on the actions that lead to my father's deportation. I saw I had a choice that night: I could get angry or I could transcend my pain by becoming an advocate for change. The next morning, I decided to transcend my pain and allow people in so they could understand my journey. Because if they could understand my journey, perhaps they might be better equipped to navigate their own.

I believe there's a widespread crisis of unawareness in our world today. We're so unconscious of our behaviors and biases that we regularly inflict trauma on others, even the people we care about. Norms and behaviors inherited from our environments put our souls in a constant battle between darkness and light. We can't escape the fact that these two forces will always be at odds with each other, which places conflict at the very heart of our being.

In our darkest moments, we're buried in feelings of pain, grief, regret, disappointment, and devastation. At times like these, we can't see a way out of what feels like never-ending pain. However, when you lean into the darkness, you'll see there's usually a reason things happened the way they did. Our experiences are mirrors of how we perceive ourselves, so when we have negative experiences, it's a response to a part of us that needs healing. Unconsciously, we project the image of ourselves we'd like the world to see.

To experience true darkness guides you in understanding light, which in turn gives you a better perception of the light. The two forces must be in balance to truly activate the God within. It's our birthright; the pain we feel in moments of chaos is only a stamp in time.

Understanding how we affect each other is at times the most challenging task we can undertake. With our world in such turmoil, and our minds clinging to repetitive negativity, we sometimes don't understand there's a bright light at the end of the tunnel.

Through self-reflection, I gained clarity into what my passion was and how I wanted to impact the world. One of the things I knew had to change was how I engaged with my environment. I took a mental break from life and started to put the pieces together one by one, like the characters in my stories. They were only living within the parameters of what they understood and knew. We're used to sticking to the practices that have been passed down to us through generations by people who were trying to figure out their own lives. Some of these practices are valuable for building sustainable connections, systems, and social structures, while others are not. Above all, being reflective opens the journey to activating the God within.

The different masks we wear are survival tools for our world, allowing us to move from one environment to another. When we're unaware of our masks, we run the risk of losing control of our lives in the long run. Observe your environment from a different perspective to strengthen your situational and internal awareness. The masks are fragments of our being; with deep understanding of them, you can strengthen your self-identity.

Take care of yourself—try to create the work/life balance you need to function in your career and personal life. You can't help others when you're running on empty, striving to please a world that makes you feel replaceable. When you spread yourself too thin, you can also create toxic conditions for others. Learn to practice setting healthy boundaries and only taking on as much as you can handle.

The people in our lives are mirrors to who we are deep down. Make sure the company you keep supports your growth and best interests. Giving away your power is the equivalent of letting someone make decisions for your life. Remember, you're the one in the driver's seat—don't let fear take your wheel of destiny. It's okay to stand up for yourself; once we stop giving our power away, we start to activate the God within.

We're in a continual battle between what's right for our external world versus what's morally right. Our inherited garments of traditions, cultures, perceptions, and backgrounds stem from our earliest foundations. But at times we have to retire practices that no longer serve us. Follow the inner voice within and you'll likely find your childhood passion never left you. Step back and look at your situation and ask yourself, Am I living the life I desire? At the end of the day, you have the power to make the final decision.

Life can put us in situations that subject us to extreme pain. When you get into ruts, take time to look for sustainable solutions for your problems. Band-Aids only lead to deeper issues that can escalate when overlooked. Weigh your options carefully when you come face-to-face with unexpected situations.

We all experience pain in our lives, whether it's from a breakup, a traumatic event, or unfortunate circumstances. It's our duty to ensure we don't pass the pain we experience from one situation to another. Transforming our pain for healing will produce better results. We're in a relationship with everything around us. It's our duty to make sure we take care of each other's hearts.

Chaos is all around us. It's in the news, our workplaces, even within the practices we inherited from our upbringing. And this chaos comes along with the emotional baggage we carry about the past. Taking accountability for our actions can lead to creating a better future in the long run.

Each day, I step into the world. I don't know what I'm going to experience from one day to the next; all I can hope for is a better tomorrow. Tough situations will come up, but if we can look at them from a different perspective, life begins to look like a pocketful of diamonds. You're the god with the power to change the world. Even when you feel stuck in your life, know the situation is temporary. Try not to pass negative emotions to others; every one of us has already experienced pain on multiple levels. Being thoughtful and kind to each other will guide us through each of life's lessons more quickly.

So many people are looking for connection and meaning. One of the best ways to find meaning is to look within yourself for the answers. When we do the vital work of understanding ourselves and eliminating mindless behaviors, peace sets in. Breaking through unseen barriers expands the level of our thinking, and in return, evolution sets us on the path toward our ultimate potential. We have the power to create the internal peace we seek.

Lean in and live the life you desire. *Lean into your power and leverage the magic within you.*

ABOUT MINDLESS BEHAVIORS

OVERVIEW

We are a social experiential platform that strives to build community awareness of deeply ingrained behavioral patterns that can be barriers to personal growth. Through our social experiences, we connect individuals with their inner voice to create a pathway to emotional intelligence and build a sense of identity. Our platform offers effective communication tools that enable people to increase self-awareness, enhance perceptions, and implement problem-solving tactics in everyday life.

BOOK

Mindless Behaviors brings to life thought-provoking viewpoints that are different takes on our usual way of living and approaching problems. It will help you unblock areas of your life that feel cluttered and enhance your ability to awaken the God within you.

Through my personal, professional, and social experiences, I've learned that most of life's problems are really just different versions of the same handful of problems. Undeniably, there are patterns that regularly wreak havoc on our lives. This book sheds light on the negative cycles that impact the human condition and the importance of effective communication in breaking them.

Through seven different stories that examine life through the lens of Mindless Behaviors, you'll learn that if you change the way you perceive your circumstances and actions, you have the power to change your life forever. It's my hope that you'll read this book and gain a new perspective, acknowledge your shortcomings and unconscious biases, and shed light on activating your untapped potential.

THRIVING MINDS EXPERIENCE

Inspired by the *Mindless Behaviors* book, our Thriving Minds Experience will bring us together and root out specific behaviors that keep us stuck in unconscious and unproductive patterns. By attending our workshops, retreats, and one-on-one sessions, you will learn to use powerful communication tools to navigate difficult situations in an objective, constructive manner. Our series brings you on a personalized journey of growth and self-discovery. Become confident in who you are and authentic in your setting. Discover your inner voice and break the chains of complacency holding you back in life.

MINDLESS BEHAVIORS

ABOUT THE AUTHOR

Beatrice Adenodi is a marketing guru, awareness advocate, and founder/CEO of Mirror Ink, a full-service business consulting firm based in Minneapolis. As a first-generation Nigerian-American immigrant, Beatrice had to figure everything out on her own. Over the years she built her own set of tools to overcome the challenges of life. Through her unique perspective, she has been able to help many people get out of unfortunate situations by guiding them from being reactive to reflective in their setting. A sought-after speaker, she was invited to speak on stage at Unveiled Beauty 2019 and has also been a featured guest on podcasts such as *Humans*, *The Eulogy*, and *Wild Ones*.

She was driven to create her social experiential platform Mindless Behaviors in 2014 after a tough transitional phase led her to reflect on her relationships, faith, and career. Feeling powerless and invisible, she discovered she had been ignoring her own voice and reacting without thinking in difficult situations. Beatrice set out to reclaim her power. As she grew into her voice, she realized she wasn't alone. She recognized the impact her newly reflective mindset could make on society and developed an innovative new approach to guide others to find their own voices.

With the completion of her book about these experiences, *Mindless Behaviors: Breaking through Unseen Barriers,* her platform is now poised to help create generations of hopeful people.

CPSIA information can be obtained
at www.ICGtesting.com
Printed in the USA
FSHW010350260321
79867FS